the 'vacation effect' concept and lifestyle were born, totally transforming her life forever. Now, you have the opportunity right in front of you to transform your own life, too, if you put the principles in The Vacation Effect for Entrepreneurs into action. Follow Denise's blueprint and 'make today what you want tomorrow to be.'"

—JASON CAMPBELL, co-founder of Zen Wellness
and #1 Billboard recording artist

"I used to work crazy hours all the time until my cancer scare several years ago. That forced me to learn how to get better results in less time. In *The Vacation Effect for Entrepreneurs*, Denise teaches you how to do that plus a whole lot more. She really walks her talk and gives you the step-by-step strategies to live a much happier life."

—MIKE KOENIGS, entrepreneur, bestselling
author, and CEO of The Superpower Accelerator

"What's the point of having your own business if it doesn't give you a freedom lifestyle and personal fulfillment? In *The Vacation Effect for Entrepreneurs*, Denise provides you with a brilliant roadmap for creating a life and business you'll love and be proud of. I highly recommend taking the time to read this book—it is a must for all entrepreneurs. Well done, Denise!"

—GLEN LEDWELL, co-founder of Mind Movies
and CEO of Flight Club Mastermind

The

VACATION
EFFECT®

for

ENTREPRENEURS

**Grow Your Business Even Faster
by Working Less and Having More Fun**

Denise M. Gosnell

LIONCREST
PUBLISHING

THE VACATION EFFECT® FOR ENTREPRENEURS
Grow Your Business Even Faster by Working Less and Having More Fun

The Vacation Effect®, Rocket Summary®, The Vacation Effect Lifestyle™, Someday Maybes™, Freedom is a Mindset, Not A Destination™, The Life Purpose Framework™, Power Word™, Grow by Subtraction™, The Happiness Scorecard™, and forced hyper-efficiency™ are trademarks or registered trademarks of Denise Gosnell Consulting, Inc. All rights reserved.

The author of this book does not provide business or professional advice and only offers information of a general nature to help you improve your business and your life. There is no guarantee that the principles that are covered in this book will produce any particular result for you.

Primary Illustrator: Ramin Nazer

ISBN   978-1-5445-3473-2   *Hardcover*
       978-1-5445-3472-5   *Paperback*
       978-1-5445-3474-9   *Ebook*
       978-1-5445-3757-3   *Audiobook*

*This book is dedicated to my mom, Mary Ward.
I love you beyond measure and hope you
know how grateful I am for all you have done
and how incredibly proud I am of you.*

CONTENTS

ABOUT THE AUTHOR

Denise Gosnell is a business strategist, attorney, author, and real estate investor. She owns and operates three companies in three different industries by working an average of three days per week and generates seven figures each year. She is a trusted advisor to many of the world's top entrepreneurs and has spoken on stages in eight different countries around the world.

Denise used to work eighty hours per week running her three companies until her dream home was destroyed in a house fire, which gave her a much-needed perspective shift. She then made it her mission to help herself and others create a life they love without sacrificing their income. As a result, The Vacation Effect concept and company were born.

Denise is a classic overachiever who was valedictorian of her high school class, received her bachelor's degree with summa cum laude honors in three and a half years while working a full-time job, and who also obtained her Doctor of Jurisprudence while working a full-time job. She worked for EDS (now Hewlett Packard) and Microsoft, among other companies, for ten years as a software engineer before becoming a business strategist and attorney. She then worked for a top law firm in Indianapolis for nearly four years before starting her own law firm.

For almost two decades, Denise has been an entrepreneur running her consulting business, law firm, and real estate company with her husband. She is currently a member of three different CEO mastermind groups where she gets to hang out and share ideas regularly with fellow business owners and thought leaders around the world.

Denise lives in Indiana with her husband Jake and daughter Victoria. She loves traveling the world, hiking in Sedona, spending time with family and friends, and photography. She has been to over fifty countries and has a goal of visiting all seven continents.

Denise also serves on the board of the Summitville Hope Center (summitvillehopecenter.org), a nonprofit started by her parents that is currently managed by Denise's mother, Mary Ward. When Denise is not traveling, she enjoys volunteering at the Summitville Hope Center to provide food and clothing to those in need within the community.

You can learn more about Denise on her website at *DeniseGosnell.com*.

ACKNOWLEDGMENTS

To all my fellow business owners around the world, thank you for having the talent and courage to turn your great ideas into products and services that make the world a better place. I hope the principles in this book transform your life as much as they did mine.

To my husband Jake, my daughter Victoria, and the rest of my family, you mean everything to me. You encouraged me to write this book and you still loved me even when I was a workaholic for over two decades and missed so many important family moments.

I'd like to thank my mom, Mary Ward, for all that you are and all that you have done for me and our family. I'm so proud of you for co-founding the Summitville Hope Center and for the work you do there each week to help others in need. And to my dad, Zane Ward (rest in peace), thank you for teaching me how to be an entrepreneur by thinking outside the box, never giving up, and finding the niche audience that will gladly pay for a particular item when it may seem worthless to others.

To my besties, Jynell Berkshire and Michelle Sloderbeck—you are the best friends a girl could ever ask for.

To all of my team members across all of my companies—past, present, and future—I'd like to say thank you for everything you have done to support me and my vision and to help my companies grow. I want you to know that you matter to me, and the work that you do matters to a lot of people.

Thanks to Chuck Koontz at Anderson University for believing in me and for everything you did to help me when I was just getting started in my career so long ago. We need more professors like you, and I wish you the very best in your upcoming retirement.

I owe a huge thank-you to my client and friend Joe Polish (and Genius Network), who is the best client I've ever had and has since become a dear friend. You've taught me so much about what it means to truly connect with other human beings and add value to the world.

I'm also incredibly grateful to my entrepreneur friends in the various CEO mastermind groups I participate in—for your wisdom, encouragement, and friendship, and for also giving me the opportunity to share a lot of these principles on your stages. These groups include Genius Network, Maverick 1000, War Room, and Strategic Coach, among others.

I so appreciate my Maverick friends—Yanik Silver, Todd Tzeng, Danielle Brooks, Logan Christopher, Nayia Pierrakos, and Sasha Ablitt—for being the first "beta group" to help me evaluate the principles in this book and to confirm that they could help other entrepreneurs in addition to just myself. Thank you for encouraging me to pursue this further.

I'd also like to thank Dan Sullivan and Babs Smith (co-founders of Strategic Coach) for calling me the week after my house fire back in 2011 to check on me and offer me a transformative way of looking at what I was going through. That meant the world to me and made a huge impact.

To Arianna Huffington, thank you for being one of the first global thought leaders to shine a light on the problem of workaholism and the importance of self-care when you shared your personal story in *Thrive* and in some of your presentations. It was great spending a day with you, Joe Polish, and a dozen other entrepreneurs brainstorming together when your Thrive book first came out.

To Ramin Nazer, thanks for doing a brilliant job on these book illustrations and helping convey the most important concepts in this book in such a fun and humorous way. I can't wait to work on more books with you.

Thanks to my amazing publishing team at Scribe, including my project manager Bianca Pahl, for helping me make this book a reality.

I also want to thank *anyone* and *everyone* who has ever helped me, encouraged me, worked with me, or challenged me to be better. You matter to me, and I'm forever grateful for you.

Most of all, I want to thank God for blessing me in so many ways and making anything possible. And thank you for sharing the greatest insight I've ever received, which is *"Make today what you want tomorrow to be."*

INTRODUCTION

"What do you want us to retrieve in the next five minutes before your house is destroyed?"

That's what a fireman standing at my front door asked me on June 20, 2011, as my house was burning. In that moment, I realized my life was about to change forever.

Imagine for a moment that we're at your house and there is a fireman asking you that same question. **What would you retrieve if you had just five more minutes in your house?**

Would it be photos, jewelry, or perhaps a letter from your deceased relative? Or maybe an antique gun, a box of collectibles, or something else? Whatever you would retrieve is a glimpse into your soul—a glimpse of what's really important to you.

In my case, **what surprised me more than the fire itself was how I answered the fireman's question.** There I was, with an award-winning 8,000-square-foot house that had every feature you could ever want. It was truly my dream house.

Yet when it was burning, **I asked the fireman to retrieve sentimental things for me.** Surprisingly it was none of the expensive stuff. I asked for my daughter's favorite toy, my

THE VACATION EFFECT FOR ENTREPRENEURS

wedding photos, and a blanket that my deceased grandmother gave me. I didn't ask for my fancy jewelry or the expensive artwork on the walls. Things like that can be replaced. But the sentimental things that represent the most important people in my life and my favorite memories cannot be replaced—they are simply priceless.

Prior to the fire, **I had been working eighty hours per week** running my companies. I hadn't taken a real vacation without a computer in years. I regularly stayed up late at night and worked on most weekends to make sure everything got done because I was committed to reaching that next level of growth. I also wanted to make a difference in the world.

I had been providing a wonderful lifestyle for my family: a nice home, fancy cars, and lots of material possessions. Except there was one thing missing—*me*. Sure, I was there physically, **but I was never truly present.**

Maybe you can relate to that?

So, here's the real kicker. As my house was burning, I realized that there I was, **the unhappy millionaire,** working eighty hours per week doing work I hated to pay for a bunch of stuff that I didn't even care about.

It hit me like a ton of bricks.

I mean, that's what we've always been taught to do as entrepreneurs, right? Keep working harder. Get shit done. Put in more hours. Work nights and weekends. Except on that rainy June day, I just stood there—in what seemed like a slow-motion movie—watching five firemen battle a raging fire inside my dream house.

Suddenly, none of that "work harder" philosophy that I had applied to my way of life seemed to make sense anymore. **I'd been doing things all wrong, and that had to change.**

For example, I only visited my parents a few times per year on major holidays, and rarely called to check on them. I never made time to hang out with my friends and turned down most invitations to their parties. I would also take projects to work on while attending my daughter's activities. So even though I was there with her physically, I was never really paying attention. These behaviors were simply no longer acceptable to me.

That day, **I made a vow to myself that I would never again do work that I hated,** and that I would always make time in my life for the people and causes I really cared about. But I **also vowed to find a way to have it all**—both freedom and continued business growth without having to choose one over the other.

That is not the end of the house fire story. I'll come back to the craziest part of the story later. The fire did, however, inspire me to create the Vacation Effect company and write this book.

After the fire, I became obsessed with studying efficiency and rapid growth techniques. I also stopped doing work that I hated and shifted to doing work I enjoyed. But I still hadn't figured out the seeming contradiction: **how to have plenty of free time *and* continue to grow my businesses** at the same time.

I was stuck for a few years after the fire, trying to figure that out, and it seemed impossible...until one day I went to a meditation retreat that turned out to be another critical turning point in my life.

At the retreat, **I got the insight clearly handed to me from the divine,** which led me to trying a very specific time experiment, which I'll tell you more about in Chapter 1.

The results of the experiment astounded me. **I made more money that year than I had ever made before, and I had surprisingly worked 40 percent less.** But more importantly, I was truly happy. In fact, I was the happiest I had ever been in my life.

People started to notice, asking me what I did. **So, I reverse engineered exactly what I did that worked.** This book will reveal the important details of that experiment, along with the powerful principles that were born out of it.

Here is an overview of what you'll learn:

In Chapter 1, you'll learn about the **Freedom Mindset** and how the North American business culture has brainwashed most entrepreneurs to do the exact opposite of what it takes to create a freedom lifestyle business. You'll also learn the meaning behind what I call the Vacation Effect and how you can personally benefit from its principles.

In Chapters 2–4, we'll assess where you are right now and help you **chart out your epic life.** We'll also identify some things you keep saying you'd like to do someday but never seem to have the time to get around to.

It's important to know where you are and where you want to go before you start implementing a bunch of growth and productivity hacks. After all, what's the point of being an entrepreneur and growing your business if it doesn't help you create an epic life?

Then in Chapter 5, I'll walk you through my **Life Purpose Framework** that helps you identify or refine your life purpose into something powerful and tangible. You'll then find a **Power Word** that summarizes your life purpose in a single word. Your Power Word can then be used to help you evaluate opportunities in the future and help you measure your progress.

Your Power Word is another important foundational piece to have in place before getting into all the tactical strategies that will allow you to grow your business while having incredible freedom.

In Chapter 6, we get into the meat of **how to grow by subtraction** by removing stuff from your to-do list, not adding to it. You will also learn how to make growth by subtraction an automatic and permanent part of your life.

In Chapter 7, you'll discover how to **conduct your own 30-day experiment** so you can find your own hyper-efficient sweet spot.

In Chapter 8, you'll learn **9 growth and happiness multipliers** that you need in your arsenal so that you can get more done in less time and maintain a reduced schedule if you want to.

We'll cover some powerful topics such as forced hyper-efficiency, Freedom Days and happiness stacking, goal setting and freedom planning, time hacking, and success rituals. We'll also cover effective delegation and outsourcing, standard operating procedures, advanced systems and automation, and revenue and expense optimization.

And don't worry—this isn't just a rehash of a bunch of stuff you've already heard before.

Then, in Chapter 9, you'll learn about how to implement a **Business Navigation System** that ties these various processes and strategies together into one powerful system that can accelerate your growth and make sure you're on track.

In fact, **Chapters 6–9 alone can transform your life and your business** if you let them. They summarize the best strategies I've learned in more than twenty years of trial and error and a million dollars in education.

Then in Chapter 10, you'll learn how to live what I call the **Vacation Effect Lifestyle** and combine everything you've learned in Chapters 1–9 to experience the compound effect of their overlapping synergies.

In Chapter 11, you'll learn **how to course correct when things go wrong**, because they will. Life is never perfect, and there will be setbacks, such as a health crisis, loss of a loved one, or a global pandemic that shuts down businesses around the world. But you will learn how to handle setbacks calmly and intelligently.

Then, in Chapter 12, you will learn **how to adopt an experimenter's attitude** so that life continues to get better and better all the time.

I'll finish out the book by telling you the craziest part of my house fire story that I swear you will never believe.

And since you're a busy entrepreneur who doesn't have a lot of time to waste, I've also included a **summary of the key concepts** from the book at the very end so you can skim this any time you want a quick refresher on the topics. I call this summary a **Rocket Summary.**

Imagine having a life where you can approach each day calmly and know exactly what you need to work on that will really move the needle drastically. **Imagine being able to eliminate or ignore about half of everything you spend time on** because it just isn't important in the big picture.

You'll learn how to do that and more in the pages that follow. You will learn that **your life doesn't have to be all about "work, work, work."** You don't have to stay on the hamster wheel feeling like no matter what you do, it will never be enough. And you certainly don't have to wait for a fire or other tragedy to create the life you've always dreamed of.

You can create a business that serves your life—a business that *you* own, not one that owns you.

The powerful principles that I will reveal in this book are what allow me to be a seven-figure entrepreneur who runs three companies (a coaching/training company, a law firm, and a real estate company) by working an average of just three days per week.

Plus, I'm also the mother of a teenager and a wife of twenty-eight years (and counting). So, I don't waste a lot of time—and I promise not to waste yours either.

Are you ready to stop doing 40 percent of what you're currently doing and have more fun and fulfillment in your life while your business continues to grow? If so, keep reading; we have a lot of ground to cover.

CHAPTER 1

INTRODUCING THE VACATION EFFECT

After my house fire in 2011, I had been searching for strategies that would allow me to have a lot more free time in my life for the people and activities that really matter to me, but also keep growing my businesses at the same time.

After all, **I wanted** *both* **freedom for what really matters** *and* **business growth.** I didn't want to have to choose one over the other like I had always done in the past.

For six years after the fire, I tried about everything you can think of to figure this out. For example, I tried reducing my work hours without changing anything else about how I spent my time. And my revenue went down because I was still wasting time on all the stuff that didn't matter.

I also read dozens of books and attended various conferences on business growth and productivity. I would then work seventy to eighty hours per week for a month or two and implement what I learned. My revenue would then spike temporarily from this obsessive effort. **But nothing I tried seemed to give me both time freedom and business growth** at the same time, consistently and over the long term. I would either achieve growth or extra free time, but never both.

I then attended a two-day meditation retreat in 2017 with the goal of finding a solution to that problem. A lot of my entrepreneurial friends told me that meditating regularly had helped them solve some of their biggest problems, so I wanted to learn more. I had already tried meditation a few times before but never felt like I was doing it right. So that's why I signed up to attend the meditation retreat.

The retreat was held in Boulder, Colorado, at a house that the host Jesse Elder had rented through Airbnb for us to use those two days. There were around eight people in attendance. The house sat on a steep hill and had a view of some beautiful mountains in Boulder. Jesse started the event by teaching us his specific process of meditation. He then had us do some short meditations to practice the techniques that we were learning.

Later that afternoon on the first day, Jesse then asked us to think of a question we've been wanting an answer to and told us to go outside and ask that question at the end of the meditation process. So I went outside, laid down on the cool, crisp grass, and closed my eyes. After about fifteen minutes of silence and feeling grateful for my life, I then asked myself, *"How can I have the schedule and freedom I've always wanted without sacrificing my income?"*

I then heard a crystal-clear response, much like someone whispering in my ear: *"All you have to do is decide and make today the way you want tomorrow to be."*

My arm hairs stood up when I heard this message. It truly felt like a message coming to me from God, the infinite creator of all, answering my request. I don't know for sure whether it was truly from God, or from my angels, my higher self, or something else. But no matter where that message came from, it was from a pure and loving source with my best interests at heart, trying to help me achieve everything I've dreamed of.

At that moment, I decided to create the reduced work schedule I had always wanted. I decided to set Tuesdays and Thursdays aside as days off each week for whatever would make me the happiest. I chose those two days so I could still take care of my clients without there being too big of a gap between workdays.

I had absolutely no idea how I was going to get everything done without losing a lot of money. As I mentioned previously, I had always seemed to lose money when I worked less. So, as I sat there planning out how to pull off my dream schedule, those thoughts were of course running through my mind again.

For example, I was thinking, *"How in the world am I going to take care of my coaching clients, my legal clients, and the needs of my real estate company if I'm only working on Monday, Wednesday, and Friday each week? And how could I possibly do this and not lose money?"*

As these **doubts and fears kept running through my mind,** I paused for a moment and reflected back upon the powerful message I had just received from a divine source. I simply couldn't ignore that message, but I also wanted to find a way to address my fears.

So, **I decided to make it a 30-day experiment to see what would happen.** My thinking was that taking eight days off over thirty days would be no different than taking a week's vacation during that month, which I'd done before. It felt like a safe way to move forward without committing to something permanent.

So, that night from my hotel room, **I blocked off Tuesdays and Thursdays for the next month as free days** to do whatever I wanted that would make me happy. I blocked out extra time to spend with my husband and daughter, visit my parents, spend time volunteering at their non-profit, and play piano. I also texted some of my friends and scheduled activities with them over the course of that month.

I made a list of all the meetings and appointments that I needed to reschedule to have those free days. I then started sending emails and leaving voicemails for the appointments that needed to be changed.

I got home and started taking those free days on Tuesday and Thursday each week. It forced me to get a lot more done each Monday, Wednesday, and Friday because I knew I wasn't available to work in my businesses on Tuesday and Thursday. I had to delegate more. It was painful at first.

I had to identify the most important activities that would make the biggest impact and spend my time on those. I had to focus on the 20 percent of the effort that produces 80 percent of the results (like the Pareto Principle, which I cover in detail in Chapter 6). And I had to say "no" more often to requests people made from me that they could do themselves, to things that would not produce meaningful results, or to projects that I really didn't want to do anyway. I also had to ignore a lot of unimportant details I used to waste a lot of time on, like feeling obligated to sort and respond to emails at all hours of the day and night.

As I worked through those challenges, I noticed something else. I **really enjoyed the free time** I was giving myself each Tuesday and Thursday. I hadn't taken time like that for myself since I was a kid. It was so liberating to just wake up and ask myself, *"What do I want to do today that will bring me the most joy?"*

And because my day was blocked off with nothing scheduled, I had the time to do whatever activities came to my mind, whether that be hiking, spending time with friends and family, going to the spa, learning a new skill or language, etc.

I had never really allowed myself to do that before on what otherwise would be a normal workday. It felt great.

Actually, *great* doesn't do the feeling justice.

It felt like true freedom—like I had a million dollars in the bank and all I needed to think about was what would bring me joy in that moment, because nothing else mattered more.

It was a sweet, sweet feeling.

That is, **until the guilt surfaced.**

You know, that nagging voice that tells you you're lazy if you aren't working all the time? The voice that tells you to get back to work any time you relax and do something for yourself that is fun.

All throughout the experiment, there were a lot of moments where I felt guilty that I wasn't working because it was a business day.

I had to learn how to turn down the volume on that nagging voice to the point where I couldn't hear it anymore. Whenever I had the feeling of guilt creep in, I would simply remind myself that there is nothing to feel guilty about if I'm getting the same or better results in less time, and that I'm choosing a new paradigm focused on results versus time spent.

I mean, think about it. If you can learn to get the same results from three days of work as you used to do in six days, is there anything to feel guilty about? Of course not!

Yet the problem is that **we have been brainwashed into thinking that the only way to grow a business and make a difference in the world is to work harder.**

Our business leaders keep propagating this idea as the "best way" like it's the "only" way. You have guys like the late Steve Jobs, the founder of Apple, who was obsessed with work, considered a jerk by many, and was reported to have unstable relationships with his family. Yet, he is touted as a hero in our business community and modeled after by most entrepreneurs.

And then there's Elon Musk, the founder of Tesla and SpaceX, who once tweeted, "*...nobody ever changed the world on 40 hours a week.*"

I certainly respect business leaders like that for their accomplishments, **but I totally disagree** with Elon Musk and others like him who make it sound like the *only* way to change the world or make a huge impact is to work like crazy all the time.

It's simply not true. Look at **Melitta Bentz**, a housewife in Minden, Germany, who invented the paper coffee filter and drip coffee in 1908. Melitta was searching for a way to make a cleaner cup of coffee, so she punched holes in a brass pot and used a piece of blotting paper she had ripped out of her son's school notebook to create a two-part filtration system. She then filled it with ground coffee and poured in hot water, and the resulting coffee that came out the other side into the cup was far better tasting than the grainy coffee of the past. In that one moment, the coffee filter and drip coffee were born.

Melitta went on to protect her invention by obtaining a patent for it and improved her design many times over the years through her resulting coffee company. Now, more than one hundred years later, we all benefit from Melitta Bentz's original idea each time we enjoy a cup of coffee produced from pour-over and drip coffee processes.

What I find equally impressive about Melitta is that she also believed in the importance of work-life balance and provided her employees with a five-day work week, up to three weeks of vacation per year, and a Christmas bonus. These were all quite rare in the early 1900s.

As another example, the former President of the United States **Theodore Roosevelt** expanded the powers of the President and our government with **"deep work" that he performed from 8:30 a.m. to 4:30 p.m.,** while pursuing personal interests after 4:30 p.m. President Roosevelt was responsible for pioneering some of the greatest advancements in government services for the people, and even won the Nobel Peace Prize.

And then there's the world-renowned painter **Leonardo da Vinci,** who lived from 1452 to 1519 in Europe. He is often quoted as having told one of his employers, *"Men of lofty genius sometimes accomplish the most when they work the least, for their minds are occupied with their ideas and the perfection of their conceptions, to which they afterwards give form."*

It has been recorded in various historical journals that da Vinci would often work on a painting for twelve to fourteen hours a day for a few days, and then take three to four days off to think. It is clear that da Vinci **placed a high value on having time to think.**

As another example, during his painting of *The Last Supper*, da Vinci is reported to have stared at the painting for an hour, making a single stroke and then leaving for the day. It is undeniable that da Vinci's works such as *The Last Supper* and *Mona Lisa* have reached iconic status and that he is regarded as one of the greatest painters of all time.

Why is it that we never seem to hear our current business leaders modeling after the likes of Melitta Bentz, President Roosevelt, or Leonardo da Vinci?

Isn't it better to work smarter versus harder?

I certainly think so, but our well-established business culture in North America and beyond seems to ignore that fact.

Thankfully, I'm someone who is **willing to challenge the status quo** when something just doesn't make any sense. I'm also willing to find better ways to live and grow, even if it's unpopular or uncomfortable.

So even though my little scheduling experiment totally defied the business norms we are so accustomed to, **I liked having the extra time in my schedule.** I liked it so much that I expanded my 30-day experiment to sixty days, and then ninety.

I had found my new addiction. I became addicted to maintaining that reduced schedule so I could continue tasting that sweet freedom every single week.

Before I knew it, **I had formed a whole new way of life** and stopped feeling guilty about it.

During my little time experiment, **I learned that you can actually grow by subtraction—by removing things from your to-do list.** Not by adding to it.

Have you ever noticed that when you get ready to go on vacation, you get as much done in the two days right before you leave as you normally do in like a month?

Why is that?

It's because you know that you won't be available due to the vacation, so **you force yourself to focus on what matters most.** This is what I refer to as "**forced hyper-efficiency,**" where you put conditions in place to force yourself to focus on the details that matter most and ignore the details that don't.

With my little experiment, I was forcing myself to be hyper-efficient by only allowing myself to work in my businesses on Monday, Wednesday, and Friday.

I was then spending Tuesday and Thursday each week on what I now call Freedom Days to do whatever brings me joy.

It turns out that there was a double benefit to this approach:

1. I became great at prioritizing and **finishing the critical few projects that really mattered,** while ignoring or delegating everything else. This hyper-efficiency is something that most people only experience right before leaving on vacation.

2. Because of the Tuesday and Thursday free time I was giving myself, each week started to have so much joy that life felt like a perpetual vacation.

Those two principles are what led me to the name **"the Vacation Effect."**

THE VACATION EFFECT

The hyper-efficiency you experience before vacation can be a way of life.

Life should have so much joy that it feels like a perpetual vacation.

You may be thinking, *"But I don't want to take off two Freedom Days during the business week, Denise."* If you feel that way, it's OK.

The principles I reveal in this book can help you take off more days than you do now from work, whether that be freeing up your weekends for the first time ever or having a three-day weekend each week.

As I mentioned before, **I generally use my two Freedom Days during the week for whatever brings me the most joy.** I really do my best to avoid working in the trenches of my businesses on those days, but sometimes I use the time to start a new business or work on creative projects like this book that I would otherwise never have time for. Other times, I rearrange the Freedom Days as needed to travel for fun or business.

Thankfully, **I was even able to continue this schedule during the midst of the global pandemic** and some medical setbacks I faced, which I'll explain later.

To my surprise, in the year of the experiment, I ended up making the most money in my entire life up until that point—when I had worked 40 percent less. And I have continued growing and investing in my companies and evolving them to suit my life—while maintaining the three-day work week.

As a result of the experiment, I also developed what I call **The Freedom Mindset.**

Freedom is a mindset, not a destination. Freedom isn't a destination that you get to someday when you reach a certain goal.

Freedom is a decision you make. You choose to have freedom.

Isn't freedom the reason you became an entrepreneur to begin with?

As part of the Freedom Mindset, **I had to learn to free myself from the judgments of others.** I had to stop caring what other people thought of my work schedule, and whether they thought I was lazy.

I had to stop letting other people dictate my schedule and life. I thought I would lose a lot of clients in my law firm and my other companies by adopting the freedom mindset, but it turns out that I didn't.

And if I do ever lose a lot of clients or deals because of it, that's OK too. The freedom I experience from letting go of the pressure I used to feel from others is completely liberating.

Most of the pressure that we feel isn't real anyway. It is in our heads. For example, do you really think that whoever sends you an email or leaves you a voicemail expects you to respond to them within a few hours? No, they don't.

As another example, will there be dire consequences if you don't finish your to-do list each day? Probably not. Your to-do list likely contains a lot of fluff that doesn't really matter or a bunch of false deadlines that you are constantly criticizing yourself for missing. I've learned firsthand that **most of the pressure we put on ourselves is actually self-imposed**, not external.

When you implement the principle of forced hyper-efficiency in your life, it will help you cut out all the fluff. But before I help you find your own hyper-efficient sweet spot so you can create the freedom you've always dreamed of, **we first must assess where you are now and where you want to go** so you can finally make it happen for yourself automatically and permanently.

That's what we'll tackle in the following chapter.

CHAPTER 2

THE HAPPINESS SCORECARD

How often do you ever slow down from the daily grind, grind, grind and ask yourself, *"Am I truly happy? If I died right here, right now, would I feel satisfied with how I've lived my life, or would I have a lot of regrets?"*

Let's stop for a moment and really think about those questions.

In fact, please physically write your answers down somewhere—whether that's right on this page, on a separate sheet of paper, or in a journal. Keep your paper or journal handy, too; you'll be asked to write in it throughout the rest of the book.

Answer the following questions:

Am I truly happy with my life?

If I died right now, would I be satisfied with how I've lived my life, or would I have a lot of regrets?

Am I happy with what I wrote above or are there aspects I'd like to change?

I wasn't truly happy with my life until a few years ago. I told you my story previously about how my house fire revealed how unhappy I really was deep down.

I had been doing a lot of work I hated for over a decade (which at that time was writing patents for my law firm). I worked twelve hours per day, six to seven days per week across my companies. I rarely spent time with my parents and my friends.

And when I spent time with my husband and daughter, I was always thinking about work or taking work with me everywhere I went (to restaurants, to the bookstore, or to read in the car as my husband drove). Maybe you've done some of these things before too?

That horrible day of my house fire turned out to be the best thing that ever happened to me because it taught me to put my own happiness at the forefront of everything I do.

I encourage you to do the same. Let's go deeper into how happy you really are right now. To help you measure your current level of happiness, **I've created a Happiness Scorecard where you can rate yourself in the following eight categories of life:**

1. Life Purpose
2. Business and Career
3. Time
4. Money
5. Relationships
6. Wellness

7. Home Environment

8. Adventure

When you achieve your best in a given category, I believe it is the greatest feeling of freedom you can have.

Let's look at each one of these categories in more detail and have you rate how you're doing in each of them so you can **calculate your Net Happiness Score.**

Here are the instructions for calculating your Net Happiness Score.

1. In the tables below, you will see three scores that go with each description. **Identify which description in the table resonates with you** and accurately reflects where you are in that happiness category.

2. **Then pick a score from the low, middle, or high end of that range,** depending on how strongly you feel you are at that particular score level. For example, you might pick a seven if you feel like you are at the bottom of that score level. You might pick a nine if you feel like you are really solid in that level and may even be close to reaching the next score level.

3. **Write down the score you have assigned for each category** in your journal.

4. Once you have rated yourself in each of the 8 categories of happiness, **total up all eight of the numbers.** This is your Net Happiness Score. Write it in your journal.

5. Refer to the section called **Evaluating Your Net Happiness Score** for help in interpreting your results.

Note: You can download The Happiness Scorecard as a one-page worksheet, along with the other resources mentioned in the book at DeniseGosnell.com/bookbonus.

The Happiness Scorecard™

8 Categories of Happiness	1	2	3	4	5	6	7	8	9	10	11	12	Happiness Score In This Category (1-12)
Life Purpose	You don't feel you really have a clear purpose in life.			You have some conception of your purpose but you still haven't figured it out.			You have a good sense of purpose but still need to develop it more fully.			You have a clear sense of purpose and are at ease because you live in alignment with your purpose.			
Business and Career	Because you are not really enjoying your business(es) at all, work feels burdensome.			You find enjoyment in only some of the tasks that you do in your business(es)—most tasks seem burdensome.			You enjoy most of what you do in your business(es), but still find some tasks burdensome.			You love what you do in your business(es) and rarely find yourself doing tasks you dislike.			
Time	The demands of your business(es) don't allow you to do things you enjoy.			Business demands leave only a little time for yourself—and even when you do take some time, you're still "connected."			You consistently (at least twice a month) disconnect from work to take time for yourself.			You disconnect from work every week so you can take a great deal of time for yourself.			
Money	Whether it's concerns about payroll, the mortgage, or mounting debt, each month brings money worries.			You're able to "stay afloat" nearly every month, but you generate little profit and/or savings.			Although you cover expenses and have some savings, true financial success remains elusive.			You and your family enjoy a comfortable income and lifestyle that you can sustain long-term.			
Relationships	You have virtually no strong relationships with friends and/or family.			You have some strong relationships with friends and/or family.			You enjoy a number of strong relationships with friends and/or family but would enjoy having more.			You enjoy an abundance of strong relationships with friends and/or family.			
Wellness	You find little or no time to focus on healthy habits, such as eating healthily and exercising.			You sometimes focus on healthy habits, such as eating healthily and exercising, but you're not consistent.			You focus on eating well and exercising most of the time, but you know there is room to improve.			You focus heavily and consistently on eating well and exercising.			
Home Environment	Your home environment needs so much work that you don't enjoy being there.			Although your home environment offers some positives, it's much more of an emotional drain than a positive place to recharge.			You generally find your home environment comfortable and positive, but some things need improvement.			Your positive home environment provides an inviting place to relax and recharge.			
Adventure	You don't have any adventure in your life right now.			You rarely have adventure in your life.			You often have adventure in your life.			You regularly have adventure in your life.			

Net Happiness Score™:

Please go through now and rate yourself in each of these 8 categories of happiness. Write the score for each category in your journal.

1. LIFE PURPOSE

Score	Description
1–3	You don't feel like you really have a clear purpose in life.
4–6	You have some conception of your purpose, but you still haven't figured it out.
7–9	You have a good sense of purpose but still need to develop it more fully.
10–12	You have a clear sense of purpose and are at ease because you live in alignment with your purpose.

2. BUSINESS AND CAREER

Score	Description
1–3	Because you are not really enjoying your business(es) at all, work feels burdensome.
4–6	You find enjoyment in only some of the tasks that you do in your business(es)—most tasks seem burdensome.
7–9	You enjoy most of what you do in your business(es) but still find some tasks burdensome.
10–12	You love what you do in your business(es) and rarely find yourself doing tasks you dislike.

3. TIME

Score	Description
1-3	The demands of your business(es) don't allow you to do things you enjoy.
4-6	Business demands leave only a little time for yourself—and even when you do take some time, you're still "connected."
7-9	You consistently (at least twice a month) disconnect from work to take time for yourself.
10-12	You disconnect from work every week so you can take a great deal of time for yourself.

4. MONEY

Score	Description
1-3	Whether you have concerns about payroll, the mortgage, or mounting debt, each month brings money worries.
4-6	You're able to "stay afloat" nearly every month, but you generate little profit and/or savings.
7-9	Although you cover expenses and have some savings, true financial success remains elusive.
10-12	You and your family enjoy a comfortable income and lifestyle that you can sustain long term.

5. RELATIONSHIPS

Score	Description
1-3	You have virtually no strong relationships with friends and/or family.
4-6	You have some strong relationships with friends and/or family.
7-9	You enjoy a number of strong relationships with friends and/or family but would enjoy having more.
10-12	You enjoy an abundance of strong relationships with friends and/or family.

6. WELLNESS

Score	Description
1-3	You find little or no time to focus on healthy habits, such as eating healthily and exercising.
4-6	You sometimes focus on healthy habits, such as eating healthily and exercising, but you're not consistent.
7-9	You focus on eating well and exercising most of the time, but you know there is room to improve.
10-12	You focus heavily and consistently on eating well and exercising.

7. HOME ENVIRONMENT

Score	Description
1-3	Your home environment needs so much work that you don't enjoy being there.
4-6	Although your home environment offers some positives, it's much more of an emotional drain than a positive place to recharge.
7-9	You generally find your home environment comfortable and positive, but some things need improvement.
10-12	Your positive home environment provides an inviting place to relax and recharge.

8. ADVENTURE

Score	Description
1-3	You don't have any adventure in your life right now.
4-6	You rarely have adventure in your life.
7-9	You often have adventure in your life.
10-12	You regularly have adventure in your life.

When finished, add your score from each category to get your **Net Happiness Score.**

Evaluating Your Net Happiness Score™

If you scored **70 or higher**, you already have an incredible life and are extremely happy in almost every way, needing just a few improvements to take your happiness to the next level.

If you scored **50-69**, you are living a very good life already and are generally happy, but there are still several things you can do to make life exceptional.

If you scored **30-49**, you have a decent life but aren't very happy in a lot of areas, so there are several things you want to change and/or improve.

If you scored **8-29**, you are pretty unhappy in most areas of life and have substantial room for improvement.

EVALUATING YOUR NET HAPPINESS SCORE

If you scored 70 or higher, you already have an incredible life and are extremely happy in almost every way, needing just a few improvements to take your happiness to the next level.

If you scored 50–69, you are living a very good life already and are generally happy, but there are still several things you can do to make life exceptional.

If you scored 30–49, you have a decent life but aren't very happy in a lot of areas, so there are several things you want to change and/or improve.

If you scored 8–29, you are pretty unhappy in most areas of life and have substantial room for improvement.

Are you surprised at how you scored in this Happiness Assessment or is this about what you expected? If your Net Happiness Score is lower than you would like, don't be too hard on yourself. You can't expect to improve something unless you are willing to measure it. Now you have a starting point to measure from.

Let's do one more exercise that is an important part of being honest with yourself as you work towards creating your ideal life. Remember back in the intro when I asked you what you would retrieve if you just had five more minutes in your house? Write down your answer.

What I would retrieve if I had just five more minutes in my house?

We'll come back to how you answered in a minute, but I need to ask you another important question.

Why did you become an entrepreneur to begin with?

For most people, it was to have more money, unlimited potential, freedom to do what you want, the ability to be creative, and/or the desire to make a bigger impact in the world. Whatever they are, write your reasons down.

Now take a look at what you wrote for both questions. As an entrepreneur, **which are you actually implementing in your life? Are you living in alignment with your true priorities** (on what you wrote down from the house fire question)?

If you're like most entrepreneurs, you're probably doing a pretty good job in some areas (like unlimited growth potential) and neglecting others (like time/freedom).

If you haven't quite claimed the freedom that you deserve as an entrepreneur, **let this be your wake-up call.** Don't wait for a disaster to strike first. Remember that freedom is a mindset, not a destination you get to someday.

Today is the day to claim that freedom once and for all. I'm going to help you by giving you all the tools, strategies, and mindset shifts that you need to pull it off without sacrificing business growth.

The next step in that process is to help you identify what I call your "Someday Maybes," which we'll cover in Chapter 3.

CHAPTER 3

QUIT LYING TO YOURSELF

It's Time to Face Your Someday Maybes

If I had a dollar for all the times I used to tell myself, *"Someday when I have more [time, money], I'll do [the thing I want to do],"* I'd be a freakin' billionaire.

Have you ever said that to yourself? Of course, you have. I think pretty much every human has said that to themselves before.

Do either of these sound familiar:

- Someday, when I have more money, I'll travel to more places.
- Someday, when I have more time, I'll spend it with friends, family, and on causes I care about.

I call these the Someday Maybes.

To me, Someday Maybes are **future joy that you're depriving yourself of now** for no good reason. Trust me, I get it. You've been too busy to get around to them, and the years just flew by. So, it simply hasn't been a priority. And there is no shame in that.

But let me ask you an important question. If you don't get around to doing those things that would bring you joy now, **when will you ever truly do them?**

If you're being honest, probably *never*, unless something drastic changes. You will probably either die first, or you will finally get around to them in your old age when you don't have the health or money to truly enjoy them as much as when you were younger.

After my house fire incident, I learned that **someday is not a day of the week.**

That is why I recommend that you either decide right here, right now, to bring those Someday Maybes into today or give yourself permission to let them go and send them to the black hole.

Take a moment now and **write down all of the Someday Maybes you've told yourself before.** For example: someday when I have [more time, money, etc.] I will [do the thing].

Here are a few examples of Someday Maybes that I used to have on my list—to help get you started:

- Someday, when I have more time, I'll hang out with my parents and my friends more.
- Someday, when I have more money, I'll buy a second home in a cool location.
- Someday, when I have more time, I'll spend at least a month abroad each year.
- Someday, when I have more time, I'll start playing piano again.
- Someday, when I have more time, I'll learn to become a better cook.
- Someday, when I have more time, I'll donate time to my parents' nonprofit and other causes I care about.

Now, look at what you wrote down. It's time to be brutally honest with yourself. **When do you truly think you will ever get around to doing those things?**

Look, I know that you would probably rather jump ahead to the later chapters where I share all the strategies and tactics that will help you grow your business even faster and take more time off. And we'll get to that. But this exercise is part of the critical foundational work we need to do first so that when you get there, you'll know what to do with all that free time.

I'm your friend who is calling you on this bullshit like I once did for myself. I'm going to help you take action on this right now and make some decisions that could bring a lot more joy into your life. Or, at least you'll cut off some of the baggage you have been carrying around in the lies you keep telling yourself.

So, it's decision time. Please refer to your Someday Maybe list and divide them into two lists: the *keepers* and the *losers*. The things you still really want to do should go on the keeper list. The ones you care less about should go on the losers list.

For me, the keepers were:

- Hang out with my friends and family more often
- Buy the second home
- Spend at least a month living abroad each year
- Regularly spend time working at my parents' nonprofit
- Start playing piano again

The loser on my list was learning to be a better cook. In doing this Someday Maybe exercise, I realized that I don't really want to become a better cook. I don't really enjoy cooking other than with family over the holidays. I always had it on my list because I felt like I "should" do it. But I'd really prefer to let people who enjoy cooking prepare the meals for me (like a chef, my husband, etc.).

Are there any you are still undecided about? If so, what do you think is causing you confusion? As my dad used to say, "It's time to shit or get off the pot." If not now, when?

So just *decide*. Is it a keeper or is it a loser?

Now that you have a list of the keepers (Someday Maybes) that are important to you, let's brainstorm some ways you can start incorporating them into your life *now*.

Let's assume that in the later chapters, I'm going to help you carve out a lot more free time. So, assuming that you have extra free time to work with, **what parts of those Someday Maybes can you start doing now** (like this week, and next week)?

Let me give you a few examples:

Important Activity (from Keeper List)	Next Step
Spend more time with friends and family	Text a friend and set a lunch or dinner date
Donate more time to charity	Research charities in my area that have a mission I deeply care about
Travel more often	Research somewhere you can afford to travel to now and put a tentative date on your calendar.

As you can see in the list of examples, even if you can't afford to do everything you want on the activity yet, there is still some joyful aspect of the activity you can start doing right now (like this week).

Now, it's your turn. **Look at your Someday Maybes from the keeper list** and assign a next step to each of them. Make it something that is easy to do, assuming you have the time already freed up.

I recommend that you **add a weekly recurring appointment to your calendar right now,** so you have at least one hour set aside for these activities each week. You can name the appointment whatever you want, but here are some ideas:

- Fun Activity
- "Someday Is Now" Time
- The Time Is Now for Joy
- My "Someday Maybe" Time

Then, **put your list of keepers in the description of the recurring appointment** so you can refer to that list as a reminder.

Even if you don't think you can spare an hour of time each week right now, don't worry. If you apply what I'm going to share with you in later chapters, **you'll have plenty of free time as your business keeps growing.**

But before we get to those growth, productivity, and mind-set hacks, we need to create a kick-ass plan for your life that would make your life really epic. What good is all the time in the world if you don't have something meaningful to do with it?

Let's jump into Chapter 4 now and create what I refer to as your "Epic Life Plan."

CHAPTER 4

CREATING YOUR EPIC LIFE PLAN

et me ask you an important question: **How many business plans or strategic plans have you created for your business(es)?** If you're like me, probably hundreds of them.

Now, how many strategic plans have you created for your overall *life*? For me, the answer was zero—zilch—nada— until about five years ago.

If you're one of the few entrepreneurs who already has a detailed life plan that rivals the strategic plans or business plans you've created before, then congratulations!

But if you're like I was until a few short years ago, then join the club. I mean, how in the world are we so smart at certain business skills, yet so dumb in other areas of life? Think about it. Doesn't it make logical sense to have **a detailed written plan for what you want your life to be, just like you do for your business?**

Of course, it does.

Well, the good news is that today is the day you will finally **treat your overall life with the same care and attention as you do for your business.**

In just ten short minutes from now, you can have a rough draft of your very own Epic Life Plan. And if you already have one created, you can take a few minutes and refine it. Make it epic—a life that would be fulfilling on every level.

Remember how in Chapter 2 I had you calculate your Net Happiness Score in the 8 categories of happiness on your Happiness Scorecard? Well, now is where you get to **map out what your epic life will ideally look like in those areas.**

Please take a few minutes right now to **fill out the Epic Life Plan worksheets** that are available to download as part of the book bonuses, or you can just answer the questions listed in this chapter in your journal or notebook. Be as detailed as you can. What do you want to be, do, feel, or have in each of these areas?

In writing down your answers, you should also **think through the biggest obstacles** that are most likely to stand in your way of achieving that plan. Once you know the biggest obstacle, you can identify the best way to overcome it and include those actions in your plan.

As you fill in what you want your epic life to look like, don't forget to include the keepers from your Someday Maybe list from Chapter 3. You want to make sure those activities you've always wanted to do are included in your plan.

OK, it's your turn to jump in and start laying out your Epic Life Plan.

If you haven't already done so, you can download the Epic Life Plan worksheets that are included with the other bonuses for the book at *DeniseGosnell.com/bookbonus.*

Answer the questions shown in the next section for each of these 8 categories of happiness:

1. Life Purpose
2. Business and Career
3. Time
4. Money
5. Relationships
6. Wellness
7. Home Environment
8. Adventure

Questions to Ask

How did you rate yourself in your Happiness Scorecard in this particular category of happiness? Why did you assign that score?

What do you really want your life to look like in this category (to be, do, feel, or have)?

What is the biggest obstacle standing in the way of where you are right now and where you would like to be in this category? What are some ways you can overcome that obstacle?

What are the best actions you can take in the next month or quarter to move closer to this goal?

Below are a few examples of some of my answers from when I first created this exercise several years ago—just to give you some ideas. Note that I've made substantial progress since I wrote the version below. I felt my original examples would probably be the most useful to where you may be right now.

LIFE PURPOSE

How did you rate yourself in your Happiness Scorecard in this particular category of happiness? Why did you assign that score?

I rated myself a six for life purpose. I assigned that score because I'm spending too much time working on things I don't enjoy doing, and not enough time with the causes and people I really care about.

What do you really want your life to look like in this category (to be, do, feel, or have)?

I would really like to feel like I'm making a big difference in the world in both my personal life and my business.

In my personal life, I want to make sure I always have plenty of time to help others, whether that be nonprofits/causes that I care about or a friend who is in need. In my business, I want to feel like everything I'm doing in my businesses allows me to be an amplifier where I get to constantly learn new and exciting things, use what I learn to help others, and simplify complicated topics for others.

When I use my gifts, it helps more people and elevates the world. I want to wake up each day on fire and feel like I'm living my life in alignment with my purpose and where almost everything I do brings me great joy and meaning (whether personal or work). I know that not every single thing I do in life will always feel joyful, but I'd like to feel this way most of the time.

What is the biggest obstacle standing in the way of where you are right now and where you would like to be in this category? What are some ways you can overcome that obstacle?

I'm spending way too much time taking on projects I shouldn't do and that don't bring me joy. Some of them I need to stop accepting as projects for my companies, and others are ones that I should delegate to others on the team.

The best way to overcome that obstacle would be to develop criteria for when to say *yes* or *no*, and then enforce that rule as new projects come in. Another way I can overcome that obstacle is to hire another senior person with my level of experience that I could delegate some of those projects to that I don't want to do but they would absolutely love doing.

What are the best actions you can take in the next month or quarter to move closer to this goal?

The best actions I can take to move closer to this goal will be to add appointments on my calendar with the nonprofits and other causes that I care about so I can make sure I treat them with the same care and attention as my other business meetings. I can also schedule activities to meet my friends and family for lunch or dinner to make sure those happen too. And if I implement the criteria for what to say *yes* versus *no* to and hire other senior people, that will be a game changer in my work life so I'm only working on projects I enjoy.

ADVENTURE/FUN

How did you rate yourself in your Happiness Scorecard in this particular category of happiness? Why did you assign that score?

I rated myself a score of eight for adventure/fun. I assigned that score because I've done a good job of taking a vacation or trip each month to really cool locations and designing my work schedule around my hobby of traveling. I've also traveled abroad for at least one month per year, so that has been fun.

What do you really want your life to look like in this category (to be, do, feel, or have)?

I want to continue with my travel adventures in the CEO mastermind groups I participate in and in trips that I plan for myself. I love the adventure of traveling to new places and learning about new cultures. I would like to spend more time hiking in beautiful locations such as Sedona and also purchase a second home in Sedona. I would also like to start spending at least three months abroad instead of just one month abroad.

I want my life to be filled with awe and wonder every single month, and ideally every single week. This includes the wonder of Mother Earth, the wonder of the sky and other planets, and the wonder of interesting places and cultures. I also want to capture that awe and wonder through beautiful photography, since I love taking pictures and capturing the feeling of those special moments.

What is the biggest obstacle standing in the way of where you are right now and where you would like to be in this category? What are some ways you can overcome that obstacle?

The biggest obstacle standing in my way from living abroad three months per year and having even more awe and wonder in my life is finding and hiring more senior-level team members who can handle the high-level activities that I'm the only one doing currently. I can overcome that obstacle by hiring those team members.

What are the best actions you can take in the next month or quarter to move closer to this goal?

To move closer to my goal of weekly or monthly awe and wonder, I can schedule several of those types of activities multiple times per month. For example, I've heard that there are some really fun UFO tours held in Sedona. I could book one of those and learn more about the sky and see if there really are UFOs flying over Sedona. I could plan out some future adventures to other countries.

I could also look at the upcoming schedule of the CEO mastermind groups that I'm a member of and see if they have any international trips or interesting excursions on their calendar for the next twelve months. I could also sign up for some art and photography classes.

Now that you have some ideas on what you might put in your Epic Life Plan, go ahead and write yours down.

I'll be waiting for you on the other side of this chapter in a few minutes.

Congratulations on taking the time to write out your Epic Life Plan. Please take a minute to read back through it now and make sure it captures what would truly make you happy in all 8 categories of happiness.

Recommended Resource

If you ever want to go deeper in building out an Epic Life Plan, I recommend a program called Lifebook (*mindvalley. com/lifebook*). This is the program I went through several years ago that was incredibly transformative.

You'll be using this plan later as the roadmap for what to do with all the free time you're about to create. But before we get to the meat of the time and growth hacking strategies, there is one more foundational piece to put in place first.

Next, we're going to demystify this concept called "life purpose" once and for all.

You'll become crystal clear on your life purpose and will name it with a "Power Word," which is one word that summarizes your purpose.

You're really going to like Chapter 5, so let's dig in.

CHAPTER 5

IDENTIFYING YOUR LIFE PURPOSE AND POWER WORD

ave you ever asked yourself, *"What is my life purpose and how do I know if I'm living it?"*

I don't know about you, but that is a question I used to ask myself all the time. I even spent decades studying different views on this seemingly **mystical word,** *purpose*.

I learned some viewpoints that said there is one specific thing each of us is meant to do in our lifetime, and if we don't do it, we don't reach our full potential. This might be something like work to end world hunger, lead a group of people, etc. Others talked about purpose as the reason you get up in the morning or the motivating aims of your life.

To be honest, none of those definitions ever felt good to me. I wanted a definition of life purpose that made me feel good—one that I could connect with daily and use as a guiding light in my business and personal life.

I finally came up with my own definition of life purpose that really resonates with me and noticed how much peace it gave me. I turned it into what I now call the **Life Purpose Framework** and started sharing it with other friends and entrepreneurs. They loved it too, especially the simplicity of it.

I'm really excited to be sharing my Life Purpose Framework with you. I know you're probably anxious to skip ahead to the chapters with the business growth hacks, but please stick with me because it all fits together—I promise.

I believe **the primary life purpose that God intended for each of us to experience is to simply live in joy.** I also believe that God is the most loving parent of all, and that God wants us all to be happy but gives us free will to experience the consequences of our choices.

In my opinion, the best way to live in joy is to **identify your unique talents that you love doing and share them with the world.** The act of doing what you love and sharing it with others creates the joy. When each person does this, I believe we can reach the best version of society possible.

I realize that still sounds pretty vague without more structure around it. That's where my **Life Purpose Framework** comes in.

Before we dive into those details, I first want to clarify that **it's totally OK if you have different views than I do on life purpose,** based upon your particular religious views or otherwise.

Even if you disagree with my definition of life purpose, please stick with me on this, because I truly believe **there are some great insights you will gain from working through this framework** that you can combine with whatever beliefs you also have on this subject.

Now, let's look at my **Life Purpose Framework** in more detail. There are **three parts** to the framework:

1. Identify your top three unique and joyful talents.
2. Find a Power Word—a single word—that summarizes your three main talents.
3. Create your Life Purpose Statement.

Let's go through each one of these in more detail now.

STEP 1: IDENTIFY YOUR TOP THREE UNIQUE AND JOYFUL TALENTS

Before we jump in and have you do this for yourself, let's look at a few examples from other people to illustrate the concept.

Take me, for starters. Here are my **three unique and joyful talents:**

- Problem-solving/simplifying the complex
- Learning new things
- Helping others

Here are a few examples from clients I've worked with one-on-one.

Example #1:
- Communicating transformative strategies
- Problem-solving
- Making a difference

Example #2:
- Helping others (who are less fortunate) have their own transformation
- Problem-solving/fixing
- Learning new things

Example #3:
- Catalyze the catalysts
- Co-create ideas and business models
- Instigate mischief, mayhem, and magic

As you can see, these unique talents are pretty broad, and that is by design. It was very important to me that I create a **Life Purpose Framework** that was flexible enough to evolve with me as a person and a business owner.

I wanted it to reflect qualities about me that aren't specific to any one business. After all, you are not your business. **Your business is just one small expression of who you really are** and what you are capable of creating.

With those examples in mind, please take a moment now and **brainstorm three talents that you love about yourself** and will always do because they are just part of the DNA of who you are.

These are **the gifts that God gave you,** so you can do a lot of good with them in the world if you so choose.

List your unique and joyful talents.

If you wrote down more than three on your list, pick your top three. There is certainly no law that says you must stick with just three talents, but I recommend choosing three for the sake of simplicity. It becomes harder to remember them if you have too many. See if you can combine some of them if you're having a hard time picking the three that best represent you and your unique talents.

For example, in mine, I combined "problem-solving" and "simplifying the complex" into one, since they are so closely related.

To me, **your life purpose is simply to put those talents into action as much as you can.** If you do, your life will be the happiest and the most fulfilling. And you will help the most people as a result.

In other words, your purpose in life is simply to be happy, and **the most obvious way to be happy is to do things that make you happy as often as you can.** So, if you put those three talents into action as much as possible, you will be happier and live your life "on purpose."

It's really that simple.

When I finally came to that understanding, it was so liberating. I finally found a definition for life purpose that made sense to me. But something was still missing. It was still a bit cumbersome to mentally think through my three main talents each time I wanted to evaluate how well I was living my life.

So, I decided to give those three talents a single word that conveys their meaning in a powerful way.

That brings us to step two in the **Life Purpose Framework,** where we **find a single word—a Power Word—that really encompasses your three unique and joyful talents.**

STEP 2: FIND A POWER WORD THAT SUMMARIZES YOUR THREE MAIN TALENTS

For my Power Word, I came up with the word *amplifier* because an amplifier is a piece of equipment that takes in a bunch of noise (information and complexities) and outputs something beautiful for others to enjoy.

Do you see how that one word beautifully encompasses all three of my unique talents? When I'm learning new things, I must process a bunch of inputs. I then output something beautiful from those inputs when I problem-solve, simplify the complex, and help others.

Here are the Power Words for those same clients I mentioned before:

Example #1:
Igniter

- Communicating transformative strategies
- Problem-solving
- Making a difference

Example #2:

Illuminator

- Helping others (who are less fortunate) have their own transformation
- Problem-solving/fixing
- Learning new things

Example #3:

Catalyst

- Catalyze the catalysts
- Co-create ideas and business models
- Instigate mischief, mayhem, and magic

Just to give you even more ideas for yourself, here is a chart showing several Power Word examples that are common for entrepreneurs:

Power Words			
Activator	Defender	Innovator	Simplifier
Adventurer	Diplomat	Inventor	Speaker
Amplifier	Experimenter	Magnifier	Teacher
Artist	Explorer	Maker	Thinker
Catalyst	Helper	Mediator	Transformer
Collaborator	Healer	Motivator	Uplifter
Composer	Igniter	Orchestrator	Visionary
Connector	Illuminator	Peacemaker	Wayshower
Creator	Influencer	Resolver	Wizard

Now, it's your turn. Take a look at your list with your three main talents that bring you joy. Then, **look over the Power Word list** to see if any of them feel good to you. You may also think of a better word than the ones I've included as examples.

It took me about six months to discover my perfect Power Word. I was using a different word that I liked (Activator), but it wasn't really the "best" word.

Then, one day at an event I was attending—a goal-setting event hosted by Jesse Elder—I heard him say, "*I am an amplifier*" while he was describing himself. It gave me goosebumps, and I knew that was the perfect Power Word for me.

You may not get goosebumps when you find the right word. But you will know it when you hear it because **it will feel right to you.**

If you feel like you already found the perfect Power Word, then congratulations!

If not, just pick something today that is the best you can think of right now and **use it as your Power Word version 1.0.** You can always refine it over time. It may take you a while to find the right word, like it did for me. And that's OK.

Now, let's move on to Step 3 in my **Life Purpose Framework.**

STEP 3: CREATE YOUR LIFE PURPOSE STATEMENT

It's time to put everything together into a Life Purpose Statement.

Here is the formula for crafting your own Life Purpose Statement:

I am a [Power Word]. I am at my best when I'm:
- [Unique Talent #1]
- [Unique Talent #2]
- [Unique Talent #3]

Here's an example of My Life Purpose Statement.

I am an amplifier. I am at my best when I'm:
- Learning new things
- Problem-solving/simplifying the complex
- Helping others

Write down your Life Purpose Statement.

So, how does that feel?

If you're like me, it sure feels pretty darn good the first time you see your Power Word and Life Purpose Statement like that. It's also OK if you don't find the perfect Power Word just yet. As I mentioned before, it can take time to find the perfect word for yourself.

Here's what's great about having a Power Word and Life Purpose Statement: **You can use it in your everyday life in a variety of ways.**

On a personal level, you can use your Power Word to help you pick hobbies to spend your free time on, and who to spend your time with.

Similarly for your business, you can use your Power Word to:

- Help you decide what tasks to delegate versus keep for yourself
- Help you decide whether to even take on that new product, service, client, or project (based upon how well it aligns with your Power Word)

What I love about the Power Word and Life Purpose Statement is that **it can also apply to any business you ever own in the future.**

For example, here's how my Power Word and Life Purpose Statement apply to my three companies in three totally different industries:

My coaching/training company

I get to be an amplifier who:

- Problem solves/simplifies the complexities of running and growing a business while also having a great quality of life
- Helps other entrepreneurs have it all: business growth *and* time freedom
- Learns new business and lifestyle hacks on how to better serve my entrepreneur clients and help them reach their goals

My law firm

I get to be an amplifier who:

- Learns all the latest internet and corporate laws and the ways to best stay compliant
- Problem solves/simplifies the complexity of those laws into concepts and actions my clients can implement
- Helps my clients grow and expand while minimizing the risks of a lawsuit

My real estate company

I get to be an amplifier who:

- Learns the latest housing trends and how to best acquire new housing for a price that is profitable
- Problem solves/simplifies the complexities of finding a nice home for low-income people who can't afford or don't want to own their own home

- Helps people obtain affordable rental housing that otherwise couldn't afford to own their own home or don't want to

Do you see how my Power Word and Life Purpose Statement translate into all these areas and companies? Isn't this exciting?

I highly recommend that you **start using your Power Word as an integral part of your daily decision-making.** It's a great barometer to help you measure how much you're allowing yourself to live in joy.

All the best strategies and tactics in the world are totally worthless if you aren't happy as a human being.

My Power Word has changed my life forever. It's hard to properly express in words how much peace and joy it brings to finally feel like I know what I'm here to do and to have an easy way of measuring how I'm doing.

Please send an email to *dgosnell@denisegosnell.com* to let me know if you experience the same peace and joy after you put this into action.

I mentioned before how I vowed the day of my house fire that I would figure out how to have it all—business growth *and* time freedom.

In the following chapter, **I'm going to shatter the biggest lie that the American business culture has been telling you** about "the daily hustle" for way too long. Instead, I'll show you how to grow by subtraction—by removing things from your to-do list.

But before we get into the nitty-gritty of how to grow by subtraction, let's take a brief moment and recap, since we are now at the halfway point of the book.

You learned in Chapter 1 that we've been brainwashed into thinking the "grind, grind, grind" mentality is the best way to succeed, when that's not actually true. You learned how I stumbled onto the fact, with a little scheduling experiment that I did, that it is possible to grow by working less.

Then in Chapters 2–4, you rated your current happiness levels, came to terms with those Someday Maybes you never seem to get around to, and mapped out your Epic Life Plan. In Chapter 5, you identified your Life Purpose and Power Word and learned a framework you can use for the rest of your life to evaluate how well you're living in alignment with your purpose.

These important foundational pieces will help you know what to do with all the free time you'll be creating for yourself in the upcoming chapters.

Next, in Chapters 6–8, you will learn the most important business and lifestyle hacks that you can implement if you want to grow your business even faster by working less. In Chapter 9, you'll learn about how to leverage the power of a Business Navigation System for running your company and identifying whether you're on track or not.

Then, in Chapters 10–11, we'll bring everything together and look at how you can live the Vacation Effect Lifestyle and know what to do when things don't go as planned.

In Chapter 12, we'll close out our time together by exploring how to make experiments a fun and regular part of your life so life just keeps getting better and better every single year.

As you can see, we sure have covered a lot of ground so far, but it gets even better. Are you ready to learn how to grow by subtraction—by doing less?

Great. Let's jump into Chapter 6.

CHAPTER 6

HOW TO GROW BY SUBTRACTION

In this chapter, we're going to cover how to grow your business by doing less—by removing from, not adding to, your to-do list. This is what I refer to as **Grow by Subtraction.** That may sound counterintuitive, but it works! It's about focusing on the critical few efforts that will produce the greatest results.

According to the **Pareto Principle,** 80 percent of your efforts generally only produce 20 percent of the results. The reverse is also said to be true where 20 percent of your efforts are generally what produce 80 percent of the results.

So, if you truly can produce 80 percent of the results with just 20 percent of the effort, **why aren't we doing that all the time?**

It's because of the problem I discussed earlier: **we have been brainwashed** by our business culture into believing that "hard work" is better than "smart work." Our business leaders like the late Steve Jobs and Elon Musk make it seem like the only way to succeed is by working like absolute maniacs.

This has created a business culture of *grind, grind, grind*.

The Pareto Principle
(80/20 Rule)

The normal tendency in this kind of environment is to just throw more labor or resources at a problem (either your own time or someone else's). But this approach is flawed because it overlooks whether the action should even be taken at all.

Sometimes the better answer is to stop doing something and take a different approach instead, or to simply do nothing at all. But when we're so caught up in the daily hustle, we often can't see the forest for the trees. We may miss the obvious and simpler answer that is right under our noses.

And the problem isn't just based upon the brainwashing about hard work. It goes *way* deeper than that.

To start with, **there is the problem of Parkinson's Law—** where the time it takes to complete a project expands to the amount of time you have given yourself to complete it.

Have you ever noticed that if you give yourself a month to complete something, it will take a month, but if you give yourself only two days for that same project, you magically find a way to get it done in two days? That is Parkinson's Law at work.

This gives us the impression we can take as long as we need, and the result is that **practically everything takes longer than it should.**

And let's not forget about the guilt. Oh, the brain-crushing guilt you feel—like you're somehow lazy—if you're not working all...the...time... After all, we have been taught that you have to hustle—to stay crazy busy to be successful. Somehow that has become a measuring stick for our success as entrepreneurs.

I'm calling **bullshit** on all of this right now.

It is absolutely crazy for us to feel guilty about working fewer hours if we get the same results in three days as we used to do in six. Yet we still do it.

Why?

Because of the problems that I mentioned before that all compound like a ton of crumbling bricks—where you simply just cave in and work more because of all the pressure.

Sometimes, we work constantly out of habit. That's what happened to me. I was a workaholic for more than twenty years. I simply could not turn it off. Even on vacation or with family, my brain was still thinking about work. Workaholism has become the respected addiction because of our business culture, and that is really sad.

Are you a workaholic? Please be honest. Are you? Do you have an addiction to work like I did? Even if you aren't a workaholic, you will still benefit greatly from these "grow by subtraction" principles.

To me, it's a lot more impressive if you can use your brain to solve a problem elegantly and with less effort than it is to use a sledgehammer to make an opening in a brick wall. Wouldn't you rather just have the ladder to climb over the wall when all you needed was to get to the other side?

You may be wondering why I'm spending so much time on this issue. Things have gotten so far out of hand on this issue that I need to exaggerate it for you to really get the point.

I hope you can see just how deep this problem goes.

So how do we solve this problem of working harder, instead of smarter, when the odds are so deeply against us—for all the reasons I've explained?

Well, you have to **put constraints in place to force yourself to be more efficient. I call that forced hyper-efficiency,** as I mentioned briefly in Chapter 1.

You limit the amount of time you will spend on a company or project on purpose. This forces you to focus on the 20 percent of the effort that produces 80 percent of the results.

The same thing happens when you're about to go on vacation: you get a shit ton of work done in the two days before leaving because you know you won't be available. It forces you to look for the least effort that can produce the greatest results.

Have you ever done that and said, *"Man, I sure wish I could be that productive all the time."* Well, you can! One way to force this hyper-efficiency into your schedule on a regular basis is by limiting yourself to just three to four days a week "in the business" like I did.

When I started taking Tuesdays and Thursdays off most weeks as my "Freedom Days" to do whatever brought me the most joy, it served two important purposes.

First, it forced hyper-efficiency into my schedule. It made me more productive on Monday, Wednesday, and Friday since I knew I wouldn't be available on Tuesday and Thursday. It made me focus on getting faster and better results from the time that I did spend working, such as by delegating more, automating more, eliminating waste, etc.

But it also gave me free time for joyful activities, whether that was working on my Someday Maybes, doing something else that aligns with my Life Purpose Statement, writing this book, or anything else that I enjoy.

Everything I've been talking about in this chapter can be summarized as Grow by Subtraction Automatically and Permanently, which I'll explain in more detail next.

GROW BY SUBTRACTION AUTOMATICALLY AND PERMANENTLY

You **grow by subtraction** by focusing on the 20 percent of projects that will produce 80 percent of the results.

You **make it automatic** by limiting the amount of time you are willing to spend on projects, through what I call forced hyper-efficiency. This automatically forces you to focus on results versus time spent.

You then **make this workflow permanent** by replacing your newfound free time with more joyful activities, so you never want to give them up.

BY SUBTRACTION
automatically and permanently

You may recall that **I stumbled onto this grow-by-subtraction strategy by accident** after the meditation retreat I attended. I then did a little 30-day experiment that turned into a new way of life.

I still can't believe I'm able to work an average of three days per week without sacrificing my income. But I do, and I even continued with this schedule during the pandemic and health scares, which I'll explain more later.

And even if my revenue ever dips, I'll still keep taking my Freedom Days because of the multitude of benefits that they provide. I can't imagine life without them.

I finally broke my twenty-year workaholism cycle, and I'm never going back. And the good news is that I don't have to.

I learned how to have plenty of free time *and* continued business growth. It's not either/or. You can truly have *both*.

To do so, you first have to find **your own hyper-efficient sweet spot,** which you can identify by doing your own scheduling experiment. That's exactly what we're going to cover in the next chapter, "The 30-Day Hyper-Efficiency Experiment."

THE 30-DAY HYPER-EFFICIENC EXPERIMENT

"*All you have to do is decide. Make today what you want tomorrow to be.*"

As I mentioned in Chapter 1, that was the crystal-clear message I received during a meditation retreat that I attended a few years ago. That message from the divine led me to try a scheduling experiment that would forever change my life.

I'm now going to share that experiment with you in hopes that it will change your life too.

I have to warn you in advance though because **you will want to resist some of what I'm going to recommend** for you to do during this experiment. It's perfectly normal for you to feel that way. The brainwashing about the constant need to hustle runs deep, so I'd be naïve to think that one measly

chapter in my book will make it all go away. But I do hope that you are at least aware of the problem now and how deep-seated it really is. The only way you can turn those bad habits around is to recognize them first.

For your own experiment, I recommend that you give yourself permission, for just thirty days (not forever), to do a **time/scheduling experiment** where you take eight business days for the month as Freedom Days.

A Freedom Day is defined as a business day (not week-end) where you do things that bring you joy but are not *in* the trenches of your business.

Then at the end of the thirty days, you can decide whether to continue the experiment for another thirty or sixty days and beyond, go back to your old ways, or try another variation of the experiment.

What most of my clients do after the experiment is to find their own hyper-efficient sweet spot, where they work fewer days in the business than ever before and carve out more free time during the week for creative business activities and just pure fun.

The purpose of this "30-Day Hyper-Efficiency Experiment" is twofold:

1. To help you identify some inefficiencies that will rise to the top when you force hyper-efficiency into your schedule (again, this is just temporary for the experiment).

2. To help you have more free time for those Someday Maybes and other things that will bring you joy, so you can experience what true freedom is like. In other words, it's designed to help you work less and play more.

I know you may be thinking, "*I can't take off eight Freedom Days right now, Denise, because I'm in growth mode.*"

Look, I get it. I was in growth mode too. But when I did this experiment, it changed my life forever for the better—without sacrificing my businesses or my income.

Plus, if you're feeling uneasy, I've got you covered. I've built in a two-hour emergency time block on those Freedom Days to handle any emergencies that may come up. **The emergency time block is there for handling emergencies** that can't wait until the next day, such as something that will drastically damage the company's revenue or reputation and requires your personal attention.

I had to add this two-hour emergency time block to make my three-day work week sustainable long term. This emergency time block also makes it easier for you to do the 30-day experiment without feeling nervous about your business. The best way to use this emergency time block depends on the type of business you have.

For example, on my Freedom Days, if a team member or client calls or texts me about something that I feel is urgent and can't wait until tomorrow, I handle it during that emergency time block I had set aside. And if no one contacts me with an issue that I feel is an emergency, then that entire day is still totally free to use for whatever makes me happy.

Since implementing my Freedom Days, I typically have an emergency come up about once a month on my Freedom Days, so thankfully, it doesn't happen very often. But when it does, I have a spot to handle it while still maintaining freedom that is important to me.

YOUR BUSINESS WILL NOT FALL APART

Are you still feeling resistance to the idea of taking off eight business days for this experiment?

Do you truly think that your business will fall apart if you give yourself those eight days this month to optimize your schedule and find your own hyper-efficient sweet spot? I highly doubt it. As a business owner, you should have other people working for you that can keep doing their job and keep things going when you are not there, just like when you go on vacation.

But if you truly have some rare type of company like a solo doctor's office where you are the only doctor for one hundred miles and people will literally die if you aren't there, then at least **adapt this experiment to what you can do.**

I have to warn you though. **Don't expect to achieve the life-changing results if you just dip your toe in the water** and try it halfway (unless your business would truly fall apart, which 99 percent would not).

The magic truly happens when you reduce your work schedule (even temporarily) from five days down to three (i.e., 40 percent). That magic doesn't generally happen if you just reduce your work schedule by a day or a half-day (10–20 percent).

Why? Because **with just a 10–20 percent reduction, you probably won't be forced to do anything differently.** You won't learn where you are currently inefficient so you can optimize your time better in the future.

In the later chapters, I'll give you several strategies and hacks that will free up even more time in your schedule, making it easier to get as much done in three days as you used to get done in five or six.

But I'm saving them for after the experiment because **the goal here is to let the current inefficiencies rise to the top and force hyper-efficiency into your schedule.** You can then use the later strategies to optimize those inefficiencies.

In other words, the experiment is purposely designed to shake things up a bit. We'll then fix what gets stirred up, and help you find a new normal that is better than you ever imagined.

DESIGNING YOUR 30-DAY EXPERIMENT

Before we get started with designing your 30-day experiment, you should first download the worksheet.

Next, look at your calendar and identify the eight business days (or whatever number of business days) that you are going to set aside as your Freedom Days in the next month.

You may have to shift a few meetings around and do some additional task delegations to team members to make it work. But it's worth it, so I recommend you go ahead and make a note of those on your worksheet or a piece of paper.

Or perhaps you're traveling in the next thirty days, like I often do. In that case, decide whether to shift more of your Freedom Days to other weeks when you aren't traveling or whether any parts of the travel should be considered Freedom Days.

For example, as a member of a few different CEO mastermind groups, I travel regularly to their events. Some of the events are in fun locations and bring me a ton of joy. They aren't work to me. They are fun. So I count them as part of my Freedom Days. But I don't count my travel days in the air as Freedom Days, since that is not the fun part of travel for me.

You can download the worksheet for the 30-day experiment and other bonuses for the book at *DeniseGosnell. com/bookbonus.*

THE 30-DAY HYPER-EFFICIENCY EXPERIMENT

START DATE:_____
SCHEDULE:_____

Write the days of the current month below. Then, mark the 8 business days that you intend to set aside for your Freedom Days (even if you need to reschedule some appointments).

SUN	MON	TUES	WED	THURS	FRI	SAT

The 30-Day Hyper-Efficiency Experiment
(Continued)

Use the below worksheet to help you plan your experiment and to keep track of important observations.

Key Delegations To Make

Freedom Day Activities

Inefficiencies I've Discovered

Interesting Observations To Note

Joyful/Positive Observations To Note

Here's one example of what your schedule might look like if you pick Tuesday and Thursday for your normal Freedom Days during the experiment:

Example #1

SCHEDULE WITH TUESDAY AND THURSDAY AS FREEDOM DAYS

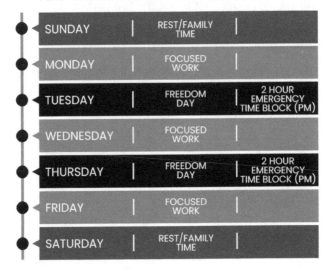

SUNDAY	REST/FAMILY TIME	
MONDAY	FOCUSED WORK	
TUESDAY	FREEDOM DAY	2 HOUR EMERGENCY TIME BLOCK (PM)
WEDNESDAY	FOCUSED WORK	
THURSDAY	FREEDOM DAY	2 HOUR EMERGENCY TIME BLOCK (PM)
FRIDAY	FOCUSED WORK	
SATURDAY	REST/FAMILY TIME	

In this example, I put the emergency time block in the afternoon on each of the Freedom Days. As a reminder, **the emergency time block is just there for handling emergencies** that can't wait until the next day. But if an emergency doesn't come up, the time is still yours.

Now, the following page shows an example of what your schedule might look like if you pick Monday and Friday as your Freedom Days.

Some of my clients have picked this schedule because they really like having a four-day weekend each week (when they are not traveling).

In this example, though, the emergency time block is Monday morning so that you could deal with any emergencies

Example #2

SCHEDULE WITH MONDAY AND FRIDAY AS FREEDOM DAYS

SUNDAY		REST/FAMILY TIME	
MONDAY		2 HOUR EMERGENCY TIME BLOCK (AM)	FREEDOM DAY
TUESDAY		FOCUSED WORK	
WEDNESDAY		FOCUSED WORK	
THURSDAY		FOCUSED WORK	
FRIDAY		FREEDOM DAY	2 HOUR EMERGENCY TIME BLOCK (PM)
SATURDAY		REST/FAMILY TIME	

from Friday and the weekend. Then, on Friday, I put the emergency time block in the afternoon/evening so you could deal with anything urgent that can't wait until next week.

You can **choose whatever Freedom Days and emergency time blocks work best for you and your business.** But hopefully these examples give you some ideas to model after.

Now, please take a moment to fill in the section of the "30-Day Hyper-Efficiency Experiment" worksheet that maps out your eight Freedom Days for the month on the calendar and marks your tentative emergency time blocks.

I recommend you go ahead and **add these Freedom Days to your calendar now** as an appointment with yourself.

FILLING UP YOUR FREEDOM DAYS

Now that you have an idea of what days you plan to take as Freedom Days and what you need to shift around to make it happen, it's time to **plan out what you will do with your free time on some of these Freedom Days.**

As a general rule, I recommend that you have one of your Freedom Days each week where you don't have anything pre-planned, and you simply wake up and say, *"What do I want to do today that will bring me the most joy?"* Then see what comes to mind.

You may come up with something that surprises you. But even if you decide to spend time on some activity you already had in mind, that's OK. **The key point here is to give yourself space for creativity and fun.**

A lot of my clients take one Freedom Day during the week for personal joy activities like outdoor activities, charity work, etc. They spend the other Freedom Day during the week on some business-related activity that brings them great joy— like writing a book or launching a new idea they would otherwise never have time for.

Please take a moment now and **brainstorm a list of ideas** (on your worksheet) for what activities you might do on your Freedom Days.

If you don't have any ideas on what to include there, refer to Chapter 3 where you listed out those Someday Maybes you'd like to keep, and Chapter 4 where you mapped out your Epic Life Plan.

Now is the point where you get to start creating your dream life—and finally make space in your life for all those joyful activities you've always put off before.

Don't worry. I promise to give you some great strategies in the next few chapters that will allow you to be so effective with your time that can get the same results in just three days versus five or six.

But I won't lie to you. The inefficiencies you discover **may be uncomfortable for two to four weeks** as you work through them and figure out how to solve them.

But if you see this experiment through, there is a beautiful land waiting on the other side of the mountain that will take your breath away with its beauty. It is the beauty that comes from living your life with more joy, richness, and freedom than you have probably ever experienced in your life.

My sincere hope is that you taste this sweet freedom during your 30-day experiment and then extend your experiment for sixty days and beyond so that it becomes a new way of life.

But you certainly don't have to. That decision is always up to you and what best suits your life. You will learn so much from the experiment about how you spend your time and where you are inefficient. No matter what, you will still get enormous value from just thirty days—if that's all you do.

The free time you spend on your Epic Life Plan and Someday Maybes are just the icing on the cake.

Here's a **mantra** I learned from my friend Karen Waksman that you can adopt during your experiment and beyond if it serves you: *"I play, I play, and I work."*

See how playful this motto is and how it focuses on play as much as work?

Another mantra that I say regularly is this: *"OK, God, please surprise and delight me today. I'm ready."*

Pick whatever mantra you like best. But the key point is to have fun with this experiment.

TO SHARE OR NOT TO SHARE

You may be wondering whether to tell your team members about this experiment and your Freedom Days. That is up to you. After all, you are the boss. You don't have to justify your schedule to them.

If you do tell your team, you can tell them you are doing a 30-day experiment that is designed to help you improve your productivity and identify time you're wasting by forcing you to delegate and eliminate. **Most of my clients tell their team about the experiment** and have their team hold them accountable to making it happen.

And remember, the main point of this experiment is to teach you how to grow by subtraction *automatically* by limiting the amount of time you allow yourself to spend on your work, which forces you to focus on results versus time spent.

It may feel a little uncomfortable in the beginning, and that is perfectly normal. For example, I felt a little guilty in the beginning whenever I had a Freedom Day. I felt like I should be working. But I stuck with the experiment, and each Freedom Day got a little easier.

Plus, I started having more fun than I had experienced in years. I started to unwind and enjoy myself. And I also quickly learned just how much time I was wasting on unimportant things. And that is what likely will happen for you, too, if you fully embrace the process.

So, let's get going on your 30-day experiment. Make sure you take note of the inefficiencies and joys you experience along the way.

The next chapter will cover some advanced business and lifestyle hacks that will help you optimize everything you do, including all those inefficiencies that you identify during your experiment. Before you know it, you will be a high-performance machine.

Isn't this exciting?

CHAPTER 8

MULTIPLIERS TO HELP YOU GROW BY SUBTRACTION AUTOMATICALLY

As you go through your 30-Day Hyper-Efficiency Experiment, **inefficiencies will soon emerge**, exposing areas that you'll need to optimize on your quest to grow by subtraction automatically and permanently. You want every minute that you're working in your business to really count.

You may be thinking, *"That sounds good, Denise, but how do I pull this off in reality?"*

Well, by **supercharging some of the strategies you've used before** and implementing some new ones too.

In this chapter, I'll walk you through nine strategies that you can combine to make growth by subtraction happen automatically and permanently. I call these strategies **The 9 Growth and Happiness Multipliers:**

- Multiplier #1: Forced Hyper-Efficiency
- Multiplier #2: Freedom Days and Happiness Stacking
- Multiplier #3: Goal Setting and Freedom Planning
- Multiplier #4: Time Hacking
- Multiplier #5: Success Rituals
- Multiplier #6: Effective Delegation and Outsourcing
- Multiplier #7: Standard Operating Procedures
- Multiplier #8: Advanced Systems and Automation
- Multiplier #9: Revenue and Expense Optimization

Most business owners do a good job in a few of these areas, but **rarely do I meet someone who is doing well in** *all* **of these areas.** During your 30-day Hyper-Efficiency Experiment, you will identify which of these you are implementing well already and which ones need the most improvement. I recommend you start with improving the ones where you are the weakest.

Once you put these 9 growth and happiness multipliers into action, you can create the freedom and business growth that you've always wanted, without having to pick one over the other.

For any of these multipliers that you feel have already been implemented successfully, you can **use these ideas to uplevel what you're already doing.**

Let's jump right into these multipliers:

MULTIPLIER #1: FORCED HYPER-EFFICIENCY

We already covered forced hyper-efficiency in Chapter 6 on how to grow by subtraction, but it's so important that it's worth including as a separate multiplier.

As previously discussed, **the best example of forced hyper-efficiency is when you're about to go on vacation.** When you get ready to go on vacation, you're somehow capable of doing like a month's worth of work in the two days before you leave. Why is that? It's because you know you're not going to be available, so you force yourself to focus on what matters most.

Remember this illustration from Chapter 6 on forced hyper-efficiency (where the man is being chased by the alligator)? He is swimming a lot faster because of the conditions he is under.

This is a more extreme example, but you get the point.

You can also use forced hyper-efficiency in your everyday life by limiting the amount of time you're willing to work in any given week.

As you already know, **I do this by giving myself at least eight Freedom Days per month.** Most months I do this by working three days per week in the trenches of my companies. Other months I do this by taking a week or two vacation during that month. By doing so, this forces me to focus on getting *results* with the time I spend working, and to eliminate the stuff that doesn't matter.

MULTIPLIER #2: FREEDOM DAYS AND HAPPINESS STACKING

You already learned about Freedom Days in the "30-Day Hyper-Efficiency Experiment" chapter. As a recap, Freedom Days are business days that you set aside for activities that bring you joy, and that ideally are not in the trenches of your day-to-day business.

But the topic of Freedom Days is also important enough to include as its own separate multiplier. You may think it's strange for me to include Freedom Days as one of the 9 growth and happiness multipliers, but working less and having more fun is key to building a sustainable business that grows without your constant presence.

Disclaimer: I can't promise you that by working a lot less, you will start making more money than you've ever made before, or that you'll keep the same income. That's not what I mean here. If all you do is simply work less without doing anything else differently, your revenue will likely go down. What I'm referring to is the **magical combination of Freedom Days plus forced hyper-efficiency,** when you apply them correctly.

The forced hyper-efficiency helped me focus on what really mattered most in the business because I started limiting the time I was willing to work. And by giving myself the free time I had always wanted, I had so much more fun that it motivated me to learn to be more effective with the time I spent working. One feeds the other.

In fact, **forced hyper-efficiency and Freedom Days are just two sides of the same coin.**

Ideally, a **Freedom Day should be where you work on those Someday Maybes** that you identified in Chapter 3. You can also use your Freedom Days for business creativity, pursuing your other hobbies, just living life, and giving yourself more time to think.

Here's another tip on how to make your Freedom Days a lot of fun. I recommend that you **use happiness stacking whenever possible.** Happiness stacking means doing multiple things together that would make you happy.

For example, if you love the outdoors and certain kinds of food, you might spend a Freedom Day going on a hike and having a picnic lunch where you enjoy your favorite foods. As another example, if you love cooking and playing cards, you might host a dinner with friends where you play cards.

For me, I love spending my Freedom Days traveling and enjoying great food, hiking while visualizing my ideal life, or visiting friends and family while playing games.

Now that you understand the importance of forced hyper-efficiency and Freedom Days, let's look at several multipliers that will show you how to be "effective" with the time you do spend working.

MULTIPLIER #3: GOAL SETTING AND FREEDOM PLANNING

It's so important to plan how you will spend your time to reach your goals and desired levels of freedom, yet so many people aren't effective at this. It's like trying to navigate somewhere without a map, and then wondering why you ended up in the wrong city.

Have you ever set a goal that involved reaching a certain revenue level or achieving a certain milestone **and then missed it?** I think pretty much everyone has experienced that problem before.

But the bigger question when you missed your goal is *"Why didn't I hit it? I worked my ass off and still didn't hit it."* I used to ask myself that question all the time. Before my house fire, I was working my ass off, eighty hours per week, but never seemed to hit my goals in a consistent and predictable manner.

After extensive trial and error and studying tons of performance and business growth programs, I finally figured it out: I wasn't spending my time on the right things. Four key strategies were lacking in my planning and which are essential to achieving continued growth and freedom.

- **Planning Strategy #1**: A system for making consistent progress on your Epic Life Plan
- **Planning Strategy #2**: A system for making consistent progress on implementing the 9 multipliers
- **Planning Strategy #3**: An effective method for planning bigger goals and breaking them down into the steps that will lead to real results
- **Planning Strategy #4**: An effective strategy for deciding how to spend your time each day on things that produce real results (versus jumping around all the time)

In my paid coaching programs, I teach my clients how to implement these four planning strategies using the proprietary tools that I've developed: the Monthly Freedom Planner, the Weekly Freedom Planner, the Daily Freedom Planner, and the Goal Setting Worksheet.

I'll summarize some of the key principles from those worksheets for you in this multiplier.

To implement planning strategy #1 and make consistent progress on your Epic Life Plan that you created in Chapter 4, you simply **evaluate your progress** weekly and monthly. You then determine what steps you can take that month or that week to get you closer to your goal, and make sure to do them.

For example, prior to my fire, I was 100 percent laser-focused on my business goals and wondered why I never seemed to achieve the freedom and fulfillment I had dreamed of. In hindsight, it's obvious. I was never spending time evaluating what I really wanted and then taking at least one step every week towards making my dreams happen. Most entrepreneurs I've met are guilty of this too.

Yet, once I started making my freedom and fulfillment a priority and planning it weekly along with my business goals, my dreams finally started coming true. You've likely heard the expression: "What you focus on expands." When you focus on your Epic Life Plan each week, you get closer to making it happen.

For the same reasons, it is also important that you **make weekly progress** on each of the 9 growth and happiness multipliers, which is planning strategy #2. To build a business that doesn't depend on your constant presence, you should always be improving with these multipliers each week.

As part of your weekly planning, you can simply write down these 9 multipliers, and jot down your action items for the week that will allow you to make progress in each of those areas. And then actually *do* those things you wrote down. They won't magically get done on their own.

With planning strategy #3, you need a way to **plan out your bigger goals** and break them down into the steps that will lead to real results.

To do this, you start by mapping out your goals at a high level, and then go deeper on each one by specifying some of the ways you can accomplish each of those goals.

This allows you to see what actions to take to have success in a given category.

I've included an example of a filled-out version from my Goal Setting Worksheet on the following page that I normally only share with paying clients; I really want to help you with implementing this principle.

As you can see in the example on the Goal Setting Worksheet, if you jumped around the chart and completed tasks under 1B, some under 2A, some under 3C, and maybe a few under 1A, do you think the results will add up? They won't. You'd be jumping around too much, and as a result it wouldn't add up to success in any area.

That is what I had been doing. I was jumping around way too much instead of focusing on one or two areas and finishing them, and then focusing on the others.

Goal Setting Worksheet

Date: _____

VE THE VACATION EFFECT

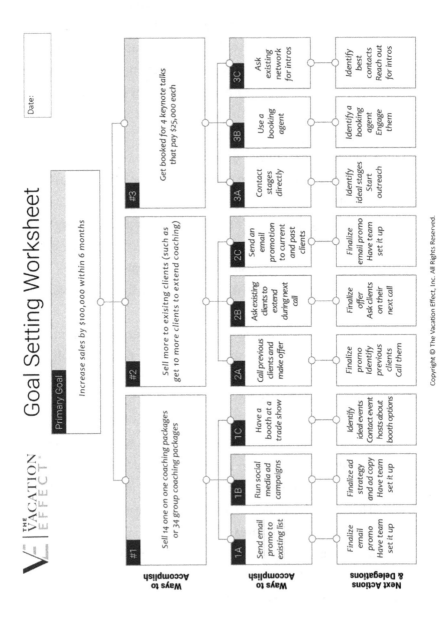

Primary Goal

Increase sales by $100,000 within 6 months

Ways to Accomplish

#1 Sell 14 one on one coaching packages or 34 group coaching packages

#2 Sell more to exisitng clients (such as get 10 more clients to extend coaching)

#3 Get booked for 4 keynote talks that pay $25,000 each

Ways to Accomplish

1A Send email promo to existing list

1B Run social media ad campaigns

1C Have a booth at a trade show

2A Call previous clients and make offer

2B Ask existing clients to extend during next call

2C Send an email promotion to current and past clients

3A Contact stages directly

3B Use a booking agent

3C Ask existing network for intros

Next Actions & Delegations

1A Finalize email promo / Have team set it up

1B Finalize ad strategy and ad copy / Have team set it up

1C Identify ideal events / Contact event hosts about booth options

2A Finalize promo / Identify previous clients / Call them

2B Finalize offer / Ask clients on their next call

2C Finalize email promo / Have team set it up

3A Identify ideal stages / Start outreach

3B Identify a booking agent / Engage them

3C Identify best contacts / Reach out for intros

For example, I had a bad habit of working on three new pieces of content at once, instead of finishing one and then doing the next. Or, I would jump around on different revenue-generating activities, such as follow-ups, reviewing new ads, and researching new approaches, but none of them were ever implemented deeply enough to achieve meaningful results.

Once I realized that my approach was the problem, everything changed. I finally started achieving tangible results on a consistent basis and started meeting my goals.

Now, back to the example diagram. If you want to have real success, it is important that you focus on completing everything under a particular branch/objective in the tree (such as 1A) if you want to have success with that branch/objective.

It's also critically important for you to have a monthly, weekly, and daily **ritual for prioritizing your day** and ensuring that you're making progress on your goals and working on the right things. This is planning strategy #4.

The process for this strategy was a complete game-changer for me. If I had to choose just one, this one would be my favorite.

You start by doing a brain dump of all the important tasks you need to get done that day. The next step is to identify which of the items on the list could be done in the least amount of time but would have the greatest impact on your business (apply the Pareto Principle here). This is something that is unique to my process that I've never seen taught anywhere else.

Look over your task list and determine which two to three activities will require the least amount of work but will produce the greatest impact. Maybe it's not exactly

80/20 percentages, and that's OK. You are just looking for the leverage points and should mark those.

Once you've identified those levers, it's time to do another part of my daily planning process that is really unique. You **assign a time hack to each of the activities on the list** (including those you marked as a key lever). A time hack is a strategy that is designed to help you get the task done even faster, such as delegating the task, doing it in batches, etc.

I go into more detail on time hacking in multiplier #4.

The key point here is that you **go through and assign a time hack to each of the tasks in your daily task list.** Then, you can go back and put a ranking order on all of them to specify what order you plan to complete them. After you do them in that ranking order, sit back and watch your productivity skyrocket.

Just to give you a few examples, on my daily task list, I will often find three to five things to delegate, a few unimportant things to delete, and several things to batch together (like email responses). I also identify some items on the list that I really want to magnetize by stating a special intention before I complete the task, such as "I intend to complete this task faster and better than I ever imagined."

I also look for any task that I can use anchoring to implement, which is a special ritual that helps me achieve this type of task more easily. As one example of anchoring, when I work out, I have a special playlist that gives me high energy to help me push through the challenge. As another example of anchoring, when I sit down to write new content or books, I put certain essential oils into my diffuser and let those aromas fill the air and open my creativity. I'll explain more on these in the time hacking strategies covered in multiplier #4.

The bottom line is that if you start planning out your daily tasks using this incredibly effective process, you will be amazed at the results. Please try it.

Now that you have a high-level summary of my favorite and most effective planning process, let's go into more detail on some time hacks you can apply to the time hacking step in the process.

MULTIPLIER #4: TIME HACKING

As we discussed in multiplier #3, the goal when performing your daily work is to **look for that 20 percent of effort that will produce 80 percent of the results.** In other words, you should always look for ways to put the Pareto Principle into action automatically, so it just happens without relying on your willpower.

You also need to put constraints in place to deal with Parkinson's Law so you don't waste too much time on a project because you allowed it to drag out. One way to do so is by limiting the amount of time you're willing to spend on a project. Those constraints are also meant to help you avoid falling back into the grind, grind, grind mentality—to turn down the volume on "the constant hustle."

Your main goal is to work smarter, not harder. A key component of working smarter is to create time out of thin air any time you need or want to.

So, what do I mean by creating time out of thin air? It means you can get things done in less time than you ever imagined possible—much like if you waved a magic wand and manufactured time.

You do this using a process that I call Time Hacking.

I've included a list of some of my favorite time hacks for you here. If you are a coaching client of mine, you can find these time hacks on page 2 of the Daily Freedom Planner, and on the Time Hacking Checklist.

You can use these time hacks as part of the daily planning process that we covered in multiplier #3 on Goal Setting, or you can use them on a standalone basis any time you work through your task list.

Ideally, you should **skim this list for each task on your list to identify how you could complete that task faster or better.** It might seem tedious at first, but you can implement this process within a few minutes each day after a little bit of practice. And the returns are huge.

Time Hacking Strategies

1. Does this task need to be done? If no, then move on to the next task. If yes, then proceed with some of the other questions.
2. Can this be delegated to someone else? (Let other people use their gifts so they also feel great about themselves.)

3. How can I force hyper-efficiency by limiting the amount of time I spend on this? (Example: should I do this only on certain days or times?)

4. Is this something I can batch with other items on my list today or another day to get them done faster as a group (like calls, the same types of activities)?

5. What is my peak state for doing this? (When am I generally in the right state for this type of task?)

6. Should I use a timer when I work on this and set a time limit to motivate me not to waste time (i.e., to address Parkinson's Law)?

7. Should I use the ritual of stating my intention before I start this task and write down my ideal outcome? (Example: I intend to finish this faster and easier than I ever imagined and am open to better ways than I have even considered. Thank you, thank you, thank you.)

8. What time sucks could possibly stand in my way today and how can I limit, delegate, or eliminate them? (Example: email, TV, phone buzzing, etc.)

9. Is there anything I can automate about this (like adding a rule to my email inbox, etc.)?

10. Can I use anchoring (certain rituals tied to certain activities) to help me get into flow on this? For example:

    a. Looping the same album each time I'm doing this type of task (like when writing or working out).

    b. Using certain scents in a diffuser.

    c. Drinking a certain flavor of coffee as I do this activity.

Time hacking is as much of an art as it is a science, but if you use these strategies throughout your day, you can speed through your task list in no time.

MULTIPLIER #5: SUCCESS RITUALS

A success ritual is an activity that you work into your daily routine that will **add up over time and give you the desired result.**

I recommended that whenever possible, you **tie your goals to success rituals,** where you can succeed automatically, without needing a lot of willpower. For example, if your goal is to write a book, you might create a success ritual of writing 250 words per day.

That number is small enough that it is achievable. But if you do that consistently, you can look up in four months and have a finished manuscript ready for final editing.

As another example, suppose your goal is to lose one to two pounds per month. You could develop a success ritual of fifteen to twenty minutes per day of movement. "Movement" is generic enough that it can be done whether you are traveling or not, whether it is sunny or rainy, or whether it is hot or cold outside.

Here are some examples of my own success rituals: I now take my custom supplement packs as I drink my morning coffee. I used to be inconsistent with my supplements, but this fixed the problem.

I have my team members all send me a quick summary every morning when they start their day, and I read it and either give them a quick clarification or I just reply with a thumbs up. This keeps them all on the right track each day, even when I'm not working.

As another example, I often walk at a park with my mom and brother in the morning after I drop my daughter off at school. I tied my morning exercise routine to the task of taking my daughter to school, so it is more likely to happen. And by having my mom and brother waiting for me, the accountability also makes sure it happens.

The key in setting success rituals is to **pick something that (1) you can easily do no matter what** so it is "excuse-proof," and (2) **will add up over time to the desired result.** I know this sounds incredibly simple, but this simple principle can change your life if you put it into action.

MULTIPLIER #6: EFFECTIVE DELEGATION AND OUTSOURCING

To build a strong business that gives you the freedom, lifestyle, and income you deserve, **you can't do everything yourself—**something you've probably already figured out by now.

What a lot of entrepreneurs haven't often mastered, however, is what I call "effective delegation." Effective delegation is where **you have provided enough information so the team member can be successful** with the project and give you the output or result you are expecting.

When I first implemented my Tuesday and Thursday Freedom Day schedule, I had to learn to become far better at delegating. So, I did. I learned various delegation processes taught by Strategic Coach and other companies and came up with my own version that worked for me.

Here is what I now include in each task I give to someone on my team:

1. **The project description.** This covers the details of what you want them to do.
2. **What does success look like?** This gives them more context around what you want the end result to look like, what it will be used for, or how you will measure if it was done the way you wanted.
3. **The priority/deadline.**
4. **Level of creative leeway.** This is where you let them know if you want their creativity or if there is a specific format or order it must follow.
5. **Level of authority.** This is where you let them know what level of authority you are giving them. For example, are you wanting them to make the decision and sign up for the service, or present you with options? Sometimes, level of creative leeway and level of authority merge into one, but I list them out separately so they aren't missed.
6. **Is there an existing policy or procedure they should follow?**

You can also **assign keyboard shortcuts** where this list of questions appears after pressing a certain key combination or typing a certain word or acronym. For example, on my iPhone and iPad, I have it programmed to create that list every time I type the word "delegate."

You certainly don't have to use those exact six questions or word them the same way. But I highly recommend that you **start conveying this same type of information when you assign tasks to your team.** You can also have your managers do the same thing. Personally, this is the best delegation hack that I've ever discovered.

For my coaching clients, you can use The Delegation Planner and The Master Delegator worksheets to help you with this.

Now, I want to briefly mention outsourcing here too, since **outsourcing is an important part of delegation.**

You may sometimes need to outsource certain projects or roles outside the company, either on a temporary or long-term basis. That can come in the form of hiring an individual or a company as a contractor.

Some business owners have the mistaken belief that they can't afford to hire any staff and should do everything themselves.

The reality is that you can hire talented people all over the world on an outsourced basis for practically any task you can imagine for a price that nearly any business can afford.

Here are a few valuable services I have used:

- Onlinejobs.ph: English-speaking workers in the Philippines
- Fiverr.com: Freelancers for just about anything
- Upwork.com: Freelancers for just about anything
- Designpickle.com: Graphic design

The hacks for outsourcing that I've learned are threefold:

1. Use the same delegation format I mentioned before with your outsourced team as you do with your internal team whenever possible.

2. Make sure you always have a written contract with your outsourced team that transfers ownership of the work they do over to you (and covers other important terms too).

3. Have someone who works for you overseas in an opposite time zone, so that you can have a 24/7 operation. For example, when my US team finishes for the day, my team members in the Philippines start their day, and when I wake up, those tasks are done. Those tasks might include research, graphic design, video edits, writing, website changes, and more. My team members in the Philippines do a lot of the same things as my US team, just in an opposite time zone. The key point here is that by having a 24/7 operation, it helps me get faster results as a company even when I'm not working myself.

It's time for you to get busy delegating and outsourcing if you are still trying to do way too much yourself. True freedom comes from owning a business, not from having a business that owns you.

MULTIPLIER #7: STANDARD OPERATING PROCEDURES (SOPS)

A great way to give yourself incredible freedom is to **clone yourself** and what you know so others can carry that out even when you aren't working. In my companies, I refer to this as teaching them to *"Think like Denise."*

Of course, other team members will also have a lot of knowledge that should be captured too, so I don't always want them to just do it my way. The vast knowledge that you and your team have are an incredibly valuable intellectual asset of the company.

The best way to capture this knowledge is through **standard operating procedures** that document the ways certain tasks are performed.

In my experience in working with my entrepreneurial clients, over half of them had no type of policies and procedures manual, and those having some procedures still had a long way to go.

Let me be crystal clear on this. The best way to free yourself from the trenches of the business is to have detailed procedures for every aspect of the business so you and everyone else can be replaced.

Here is what I recommend to help you **create standard operating procedures:**

1. Any time you find yourself training or explaining something to your team, record it and ask a team member to put it into a draft procedure.
2. Pick the most critical activities in the company that you and other team members do, and have those drafts created first.
3. Update the draft procedures each time that activity or task is being performed.
4. Consider blocking off two to three days with some of your key team members with the sole purpose of creating draft procedures for the company's most critical operations.

In terms of the actual format of the policies and procedures, I recommend something like the following:

1. **Create procedures for the following categories of your business** (which are the same categories that a business in any industry can use):
   a. Marketing/Client Attraction
   b. Sales/Client Enrollment
   c. Delivery of Client Work
   d. Team
   e. Office Environment
   f. Money/Business Metrics

2. If you are saving these files on your hard drive or an online drive, **consider using a naming scheme that starts with letters,** so they sort alphabetically on your computer hard drive.

3. Also, **consider using a naming format similar to the example below** to make it easier to insert new procedures over time.
   a. Marketing/Client Attraction
      A1 Keep in Touch Strategy
         A1.1 Print & Email Newsletters
         A1.2 Periodic Gifts or Articles Mailed to Clients
         A1.3 Birthday Cards & Holiday Gifts to Clients

4. **Include a header and change log at the top of each procedure document,** to track details about who

created it, the purpose of the procedure, when it was last updated, and by whom.

If you do those things, you will be way ahead of most of the other businesses out there. You can also use various types of online software platforms available today (such as Trainual) to store your procedures instead of having them on shared drives. But the important point here is to just get them done! **Policies and procedures** = *more freedom.* That is the hack.

MULTIPLIER #8: ADVANCED SYSTEMS AND AUTOMATION

Once you have your key policies and procedures clearly documented, it becomes a lot easier to identify the areas that can be automated.

There are **four different types of automation:** people automation, template automation, software automation, and hardware automation.

Let's look at each one in more detail, including how you can best leverage them in your business and life.

1. With **people automation,** you can either make something a habit yourself so it gets done automatically or you can have a standard operating procedure that your team can follow.

2. With **template automation,** you have various templates in Word documents, Google documents,

email signature footers, or other file formats where you just pull them up whenever needed to reuse them multiple times.

3. With **software automation,** you use software to complete some part of the task for you. I was a software developer for ten years before I became a business strategist and lawyer, so I've had a lot of experience using all kinds of software automation over the years, such as:

   a. Document automation, where you convert a template into something that gets filled out automatically by software—using a tool like *Formstack.com* (formerly *Webmerge.me*).

   b. Keyboard shortcuts, where you hit a certain keystroke (such as command + R) to have a certain command carried out (such as to open a certain template, export an image, etc.).

   c. Text expansion, where when you type a certain phrase and it automatically replaces the text with something else—like the six-part delegation instruction template that appears when I type the word "delegate."

   d. Batch processing of the same type of task, such as converting a group of selected Word documents into PDF documents.

   e. Software automation, where systems talk to each other to perform a series of actions (such as having your payment processing software send a command to your membership site software to create a new user login).

4. With **hardware automation**, you use physical machines such as robots to perform certain tasks for you.

I wanted to call this out as a separate category from software automation, because robotics is currently an emerging area of technology.

One of these emerging areas is **robots as a service (RaaS)** where you can rent someone else's robots for a period of time. This is making it easier to have access to robot technology without having to buy the robots yourself.

For example, some companies are using this method to have robots help fulfill orders in a fulfillment center, perform repetitive tasks on a manufacturing floor, or act as a security guard at an office location. I think the advancements in robotics are exciting. While they will replace some jobs, they will also create a lot of new ones, such as in engineering, project management, and workflow optimization.

I know this may not apply to your company just yet, but I at least wanted you to be aware that this type of technology is becoming increasingly popular, especially in fields like manufacturing and fulfillment.

MULTIPLIER #9: REVENUE AND EXPENSE OPTIMIZATION

Revenue and Expense Optimization is where you look for ways to increase your revenue and cut your expenses. This is an important strategy for you to revisit periodically so you can really optimize the profitability and growth of your business over the long term.

Here are some examples of ways to **increase revenue:**

- **You can always raise your prices** so there is a higher profit per sale. I've found that many businesses wait too long to raise their prices—when the demand is high enough that customers would easily pay more.

- Another way to increase your revenue is to **increase your overall sales conversions** so more revenue comes in the door.

- **Another often overlooked way to increase revenue is turning one-time revenue into recurring revenue by converting the product or service into a subscription.**

Here are some ways you can **cut expenses:**

- A great way to cut expenses is to **look for subscriptions you can cancel** that aren't needed or that can be consolidated with other subscriptions.

- Another way to cut expenses is to **periodically renegotiate contracts with vendors.** I do this once per year with my vendors, where I revisit what is fair for what I need.

- Another great strategy you can use to cut your expenses is to figure out how to **turn existing expenses into profit centers.** The way this works is that you can look at some of your biggest expenses and ask yourself if there is any part you could convert into a profit center, like renting out some time of any underutilized employees to my clients or friends.

- Another way you can cut your expenses is to find ways to reduce your taxes, such as **using some creative tax planning.** Here are some examples:
  - Renting your own home to your business for up to fourteen days under the Augusta Rule
  - Having a home office accountable plan
  - Setting up a pre-tax health insurance plan using 401k/IRA pre-tax to reduce your taxes owed
  - Moving to a state with lower state income or corporate income taxes
  - Converting your entity type to a different entity type that has lower taxes

There are countless ways you can increase your revenue and cut your expenses. If you want an incredible list of ideas, you should **check out the book called** *Double Your Profits in 6 Months or Less* **by Bob Fifer.** It's an older book, but its principles are still relevant today.

The key point here is to always be mindful of optimizing your revenue and your expenses. By doing so, it will further support you and your goal of having plenty of freedom while your business continues to be profitable.

The growth and happiness multipliers covered in this chapter can totally **transform your life and your business** if you put them into action.

In Chapter 9, we'll cover a powerful strategy you can use to bring these growth and happiness multipliers together in a systematic way and make sure your business is on the right track.

CHAPTER 9

IMPLEMENTING A PROPER BUSINESS NAVIGATION SYSTEM

"Um, Denise, I think we have a problem. Our merchant processing reports for the past two days show we should have $20,000 more in the bank account than what has posted. I don't know where that money is going."

Those are the words that I heard one day from my office manager of the real estate company that my husband and I own.

It turns out that there was a problem with our merchant processing system and somehow it got switched into the wrong processing mode due to a system glitch and the transactions didn't post to our tenants' credit cards.

Thankfully, we had set up the proper reporting and internal systems to let us know about this issue quickly before it became a much bigger problem. We were able to simply repro-cess those client credit cards a few days later than scheduled.

So how does this relate to what we've been talking about? Well, in Chapter 8, you learned about 9 growth and happiness multipliers that you can optimize one by one to turn your business into a well-oiled machine.

However, **there is one final ingredient** you need to create a business that can operate without your constant presence.

You also need a "system" to carry out those processes in a coherent way within your company. It's the one thing that connects all the dots and brings everything together that we have been talking about in prior chapters.

That system is what I refer to as a "**Business Navigation System.**"

So, what exactly do I mean by a Business Navigation System? To me, a Business Navigation System is **a unified system that allows you to track the progress and health of your overall business** and make sure the right projects get done in the right order.

As part of this, you also need a way of quickly seeing the metrics that indicate whether your business is on the right track or not, much like the dashboard of your car tells you if there is a problem or if everything is operating as expected.

The fastest way to grow your business is to have focus and speed. Anything you can do to help your team focus on the right projects that will have the biggest impact, and to get those projects done as quickly as possible, will lead to faster growth.

The truth is, you can be incredibly successful in business even if you don't have a good Business Navigation System. I've made millions of dollars in the past with a pretty crappy Business Navigation System that was spread across several different software programs and processes.

But this took me and my team members a ton more effort to get the right projects done, and to see whether we were on track. We had to work twice as hard to get the same results as we do now. And I was the only one who could really decipher where we were. To maintain my reduced work schedule long-term, I had to step up my game and implement some better systems and metrics.

If you want your company to operate in the most optimal way and achieve your goals easier, **having a proper Business Navigation System is critical.** It also makes your business less dependent on you and a lot more valuable if you ever want to sell it.

You may have already heard about the concept of having a business operating system for your company, such as using the well-known Entrepreneurial Operating System (EOS) methodology taught by EOS Worldwide. It's important to set the context for how that fits into what I'm referring to here.

Those types of business operating systems that help you run your business effectively can be carried out as part of your Business Navigation System. In other words, you could implement the principles within the EOS methodology as part of the features included within your Business Navigation System.

Here are the **three key features** to include in your Business Navigation System:

- An organized way to track your goals, projects, and tasks
- A process for keeping everyone accountable and focused on the "right" projects
- Tracking of your key performance indicators

Let's look at each one of those in more detail.

FEATURE 1: AN ORGANIZED WAY TO TRACK YOUR GOALS, PROJECTS, AND TASKS

The first important feature you should have in your Business Navigation System is an organized way to track your quarterly and annual goals and then break those goals down into manageable projects. Once you break the goals down into manageable projects, you then need a method for breaking down the projects into the right tasks.

You may recall that in Chapter 8, we looked at some powerful methods you can use for goal setting and project planning. Here I'm referring to a systematic way of tracking your progress on those goals across your entire company—including all team members.

Most business owners I know don't have an effective way of doing this for the entire company. For example, they may have company projects and individual tasks assigned within a tool like Asana or Basecamp, but it is generally missing how this relates to annual and quarterly goals, and the ability to see how well you are on track with meeting the annual and quarterly goals.

This is one of the reasons **why those business owners never seem to make the progress they are hoping for.** I've been there too, and the good news is that this problem is easy to fix.

And remember how in Chapter 4 we discussed the importance of creating your Epic Life Plan as a plan for your overall life, much like you generally do with your business and project plans? I believe that it is important for your Business Navigation System to also include a way of tracking your personal progress on your own Epic Life Plan.

After all, what is the point of owning your own business if you don't make constant progress on designing a business that suits your overall life aspirations?

FEATURE 2: A PROCESS FOR KEEPING EVERYONE ACCOUNTABLE AND FOCUSED ON THE "RIGHT" PROJECTS

In addition to having an organized way of tracking your progress on your goals and projects, you also need a way to keep everyone accountable and focused on the "right" projects. When I say the "right" projects, I mean **the ones that will move the needle along for your business.** I covered some of these methods in Chapter 8 with multiplier #3 and multiplier #4.

What I'm recommending here is that you find a systematic way of making sure you and your team members **implement** methodologies where everyone can see the overall progress towards the company's key goals for the quarter and year.

For example, I shared my unique time hacking process in Chapter 8 as multiplier #4, where I recommended that you identify the top two to three levers that will produce approximately 80 percent of the results from approximately 20 percent of your efforts.

Imagine how much progress you could make in your company if your Business Navigation System includes a feature to help every team member perform this type of daily analysis with their task list so they focus on the right things. **The results can be incredible when you do this.**

FEATURE 3: TRACKING YOUR KEY PERFORMANCE INDICATORS

The third essential feature you should have in your Business Navigation System is the ability to track your key performance indicators (KPIs) so you can tangibly see the overall health of your business at a quick glance.

Below are a few examples of the types of **KPIs that most businesses need to track:**

- Number of website or business visitors
- Number of inquiries or opt-ins
- Number of proposals sent or views to a sales offer
- Current mailing list size
- Number of closed sales
- Gross sales

- Number of refunds
- Number of chargebacks

You can also include anything else that is useful to you in helping you run your business, such as any that are specific to your type of business.

Those three features—project tracking, accountability, and KPI tracking—are the bare minimum that I recommend you include so you can measure your company's progress and know whether everyone is working on the right things.

Please take a few moments right now and **brainstorm on whether there are any other features you want to include** in your Business Navigation System if you don't already have one that is comprehensive.

IMPLEMENTING YOUR BUSINESS NAVIGATION SYSTEM

As I mentioned earlier, you can implement or refine your Business Navigation System in the form of one or more software programs or even use manual processes and forms on paper as necessary. **I recommend that you implement yours using software**, ideally just one or a few programs if possible so you have a centralized view and don't have to jump around so much.

When I decided to create a better Business Navigation System for my companies, I was frustrated that I couldn't find a system out there on the market that would do everything I wanted. Each one I found was lacking one or more of the features that I wanted.

That's why I decided to have my own custom software
program built on the Notion.so platform, which is a platform
that makes it easy to build your own web-based software program without needing to be a software developer. My under-
graduate degree is in computer science, and I was a software
developer for over ten years in a prior career, so I found it fun
to customize the templates that I had built for my companies.
And my team and I are always improving them over time. My
friend and client Jon Marino showed me just how powerful
and customizable Notion can be.

As you will see in this first example, I call this "Mission
Control Center," because that's what I like to call the home
page of my Business Navigation System.

What is important about the home page of any Business
Navigation System is that it should provide a centralized view
of the key components of your business with easy access to
the more detailed pages.

In my example, you can see that some of the key performance indicators are right there at the top of the page. This lets me see at a quick glance some of the business data that is really important to monitor regularly. My system is set up so you can navigate to the full KPI page for more details if you want to see more of the data, but the home page shows just a summary of the ones that I tagged to display on the home page.

My system also allows me to quickly access the various pages for tracking my company's goals, projects, financials, and so much more. **Almost everything I need to run my business is easily accessible from my Mission Control Center.**

What's great about the Notion platform is that you can share certain parts of the system with your team and restrict access to others. For example, my team has access to the goal-tracking tools that we are all working on, but not the part that correlates everything I'm doing to make progress on my own Epic Life Plan.

This is one of the features that I couldn't find in the other software programs—none of them had an easy way for me to separately track progress on my own Epic Life Plan and relate it to my daily activities. But like I emphasized in earlier chapters, **it's important to track your progress on your Epic Life Plan just like you do with your other business planning efforts.**

As you will see in this second example from my Business Navigation System, in addition to more quick access links to the key areas of my system, it also displays data about the current inefficiencies we're working on optimizing as a company, as well as what experiments we're currently running to improve the business or in general. **I can always modify these features over time** if my team and I discover better or more useful ways to do things.

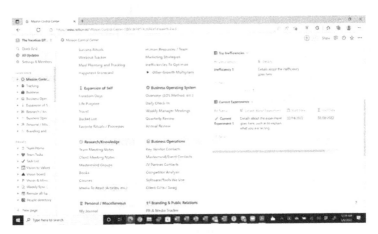

I've spent considerable time and money building out my Business Navigation System to suit my needs, but I'm so happy that I did. In fact, **I've integrated most of the principles covered in this book into my system,** such as your Life Purpose and Power Word, and tracking the inefficiencies that you are optimizing. And my system will continue to evolve over time, just like yours should.

I also provide my custom software to clients in some of my coaching programs to use and modify in their own business, or for them to just use for ideas on other features to add into the software they are already using.

I believe that access to my custom software built on the Notion platform is worth more than the price that I charge for those coaching programs. If that sounds helpful to you, **you** can apply for a behind-the-scenes tour of my coaching program and my Business Navigation System here: *DeniseGosnell. com/free-training-vip.*

I hope that gives you some ideas on what to include in your own Business Navigation System and how to go about creating one or improving the one you already have. Remember, it's all about focus and speed.

And having a proper Business Navigation System will allow you to **bring all those multipliers we looked at earlier into one coherent system** that expedites your growth.

In fact, pure magic happens in life when you combine everything we've been talking about in Chapters 1–9. That is what I call Living the Vacation Effect Lifestyle, which we'll dive into next.

CHAPTER 10

LIVING THE VACATION EFFECT LIFESTYLE

As a former workaholic who used to work seventy to eighty hours per week for more than twenty years, **it feels a bit surreal now to live what I call "the Vacation Effect Lifestyle."** It's not just some pie-in-the-sky way of life that can only work for me.

It can work for you too, like other entrepreneurs I've worked with as clients, even during the ups and downs of life and business.

But you must be willing to do things differently than you have in the past. **You must be willing to challenge the** *grind, grind, grind* **mentality** that is so prevalent in our society today.

You must be willing to stand for the principle that working smarter is better than harder, and there is nothing to feel guilty about if you get the same results in three days as you used to in six.

If you are willing to be bold and experiment with the principles learned about thus far, I'm confident you can find your own hyper-efficient sweet spot that will work best for you.

There is something truly magical that happens when you give yourself more free time and creative space. You'll bring so much more joy to your work because you'll always have something fun to look forward to each week.

You'll also **get more done in less time** than before due to the forced hyper-efficiency of limiting the time you spend working *in* the business.

Then, when you apply the 9 growth and happiness multipliers that I covered in Chapter 8, you'll become more effective than ever before. Even if you only implement some of the 9 growth and happiness multipliers, you can experience huge transformations in your life and business. If you implement all of them, the changes will be so profound that **you won't even recognize your life and business anymore** because it will be better than you ever imagined was possible.

It's kind of like what happens with a bunch of dominoes lined up in a row. You knock the first one down and it then starts a chain reaction that knocks down the rest. The first domino is when you reduce your work schedule on purpose to give yourself more free time and force yourself to stop wasting so much time. This causes you to focus on the critical few projects that produce the greatest results and to cut out all the wasted time on things that don't really matter.

This also helps you **stop feeling obligated to comply with the demands of other people** that you never actually agreed to take on, which is *huge*.

As you become happier and more effective, your employees will too. It is truly contagious.

And it's way more powerful than just a domino effect where one step causes the next one in a particular sequence. It's *sooo* much bigger than that.

What happens is a compound effect that is hard to properly convey with words, where one not only causes the other, but where they all make each other better together.

One way I try to explain the compound effect further is with this formula:

LESS WORK + FORCED HYPER-EFFICIENCY + MORE JOY = FASTER BUSINESS GROWTH

When you live the Vacation Effect Lifestyle, life has so much joy built in that each week feels like a vacation. You get to have fun integrating those "Someday Maybes" into your life that you never got around to before. You get to **start making your Epic Life Plan a part of your new reality.**

You get to experience true freedom that comes from being a business owner who has worked smarter instead of harder, while your business continues to grow. **You no longer have to wait for vacation to experience true joy.** It becomes a normal way of life.

Less Work + Forced Hyper-Efficiency + More Joy

= Faster Business Growth

This is what I referred to in earlier chapters as:

GROW BY SUBTRACTION AUTOMATICALLY AND PERMANENTLY

As I mentioned before, you **grow by subtraction** by working less than before and eliminating things from your to-do list.

You do this **automatically** by putting limits in place to force you to be hyper-efficient (like with the Freedom Day schedule and some of the other growth multipliers).

You make this **permanent** by replacing the newfound free time with things that bring you so much joy that you never want to go back to the old "grind, grind, grind" schedule again. Instead of being addicted to working, you become addicted to optimizing and having fun.

Imagine what it will feel like when you can live life from a relaxed state where you have plenty of time for what truly matters to you, and where you can approach challenges with a sense of calm. If you put these principles into action, that is truly possible for you, like it has been for me and some other business owners I've worked with who made this a way of life.

I hope you don't wait for a disaster to strike (like what happened to me) or a near-death experience before you start to embrace the freedom you deserve as an entrepreneur.

There will never be a better time than *right now* to spend time with the people, causes, and activities that really matter to you.

You truly can have it all: continued business growth and plenty of free time.

But you have to be willing to experiment with these principles and step out of your comfort zone when others may not understand why.

I've also included a cool poster for you that contains a list of the most important principles to help you implement the Vacation Effect Lifestyle. You can download a PDF of this poster as part of the bonuses that come with this book at *DeniseGosnell.com/bookbonus*.

While the Vacation Effect Lifestyle is certainly great, **it doesn't mean life will always be perfect.**

I'm not going to sit here and tell you that if you implement these principles, your problems will all magically go away. That would be a lie.

Shit will hit the fan from time to time, like we all experienced with the COVID-19 pandemic. You will have ups and downs in business and life. But when you are living the Vacation Effect Lifestyle, **you will have the time and mental space to handle those setbacks with more ease and grace.**

In the next chapter, we'll look at what to do when that happens.

CHAPTER 11

COURSE CORRECTING WHEN THINGS GO WRONG

"You need to head to the ER right now," said the doctor at the urgent care center. "Your appendix is about to rupture."

I heard those words in January 2018, just a year after I had put all the principles from this book into action. Thankfully, all went well with the surgery and I was only hospitalized for two days.

Now, fast forward to 2020 when the world was swept by the COVID-19 pandemic. Nations issued lockdowns. Businesses closed. More than six million people died over a two-year period (as of this printing). Russia invaded Ukraine, causing another war to start. These events in turn caused inflation, where the price of gas, building materials, groceries, and many other goods began to rise.

These incidents are just another reminder that no matter how much we plan and how great life may be, **there will always be a few curve balls headed our way.**

In this chapter, **we'll look at some tools and techniques you can use to handle these problems as they arise,** including when to put your Freedom Days on hold temporarily and when not to.

For example, there will likely come a time when it will feel like you should just go back to working harder, instead of smarter. **You may be tempted to give up your Freedom Days** and jump back to the way you used to operate.

Please resist that temptation and carefully **evaluate whether that really is the answer.**

Sure, things are bound to go wrong with your business in the future—sales will dip, the economy will change, you may lose a big vendor contract, you may become sick, or an employee or third party may steal something, etc.

That is sadly just part of the ups and downs of business and life.

To help you determine how to handle these situations and **protect your Freedom Days as much as possible,** I've created a framework called The Freedom Day Protector.

The Freedom Day Protector is designed to help you evaluate whether to throw more of your personal time and/or resources at a project or whether that is really the answer.

In other words, it helps you decide what to do when you are tempted to start working *in* the business fifty to sixty-plus hours again and are tempted to kill the Freedom Day idea.

Here are the key questions to ask yourself (write your answers down in your journal or on a separate piece of paper):

Part 1: Evaluate who should handle the crisis.

1. Is this something that I personally need to handle? If yes, go to Part 2. If not, skip to Part 3.

Part 2: It needs to be handled by me, personally.

1. Is throwing more of my time/resources at this truly going to solve this problem, or is there a smarter way to resolve this that doesn't involve more time?

2. Should I give up my Freedom Days this week or this month (whatever the case may be) to handle this?
3. If yes, will that really solve the problem? If so, how long will I need to set my Freedom Days aside to solve this?

There are rarely situations where giving up your Freedom Days will solve the problem any faster than if you remain calm and keep your Freedom Days.

But when that really does happen, it is OK for you to do what needs to be done to resolve the situation, even if that means temporarily putting your Freedom Days on hold to address the crisis.

Part 3: It needs to be handled by a team member.
1. Who else on the team should be handling this?
2. Do they have the resources they need to handle it?
3. If not, what else do I need to do so they have the resources they need to handle this?

I recommend that you **do everything you can to protect your Freedom Days** unless it is truly an absolute emergency that demands your personal attention. Your Freedom Days provide precious creative time that keeps you calm and thinking effectively as a leader, and also helps you sustain the work-smarter attitude.

It will be so easy to fall back into the bad habit of working all the time without being effective, unless you protect your Freedom Days like you would protect your own child.

Let me give you some **real-world examples** of how I used the Freedom Day Protector in the ups and downs of my life.

During the pandemic, I went through this exercise for myself and determined that it was worth putting my Freedom Days on hold temporarily to help those in need.

For about forty-five days, during the shutdown, I worked a lot of extra hours to help my friends, family, and clients deal with what was going on. I helped them apply for loans and grants that they qualified for, I helped them find solutions to their problems, and I just listened to their fears and encouraged them. I felt it needed to be me doing those actions versus someone on my team, although my team certainly helped where it made sense.

And **I don't feel guilty for having worked extra during that time** to do what I truly felt was best to help those I cared about the most.

After that forty-five-day period, **I continued taking my Freedom Days** throughout the pandemic. In the summer of 2020, I bought a second home in Sedona, Arizona, and I began traveling there each month on a week vacation when the events I had planned to attend for the year were canceled.

So even though I wasn't able to travel abroad for up to three months like I had planned out in my Epic Life Plan that I shared with you, I was able to buy the second home I had been dreaming of. I still travel to Sedona every month even though I'm also traveling to other events in person again. I will continue doing so as long as it brings me great joy.

Also, during the midst of the pandemic, I had another serious health scare where I was having severe neck and arm pain. There were even a few scary months where I thought I might have to stop working at the computer and file for disability benefits.

But I still kept giving myself the days off to do what I enjoy, even when I didn't know if I could keep working at the computer anymore. It turns out that I'm fine now, and some simple adjustments to my sleep pillow, my posture, and some special chiropractic adjustments eliminated the pain.

Those are examples of how **I have continued living the Vacation Effect Lifestyle even through the ups and downs of life.**

The bottom line is that I highly recommend that you **use the Freedom Day Protector** to help guard your Freedom Days as much as possible.

When it is truly necessary to deviate and work extra to handle a crisis that demands your personal attention, just do so. And don't feel guilty about it. Then get back to taking those days off again as soon as you can.

You deserve a lifetime of freedom and happiness! You just have to claim it.

And when you combine all of the principles together that we've been talking about, you can get there faster than you ever imagined possible.

It will take a little experimenting to find your own hyper-efficient sweet spot where life keeps getting better and better.

We'll cover how to set up these experiments in Chapter 12 so you can create the epic life that you've always dreamed of.

CHAPTER 12

EXPERIMENT YOUR WAY TO EXCEPTIONAL

I told you in Chapter 1 how I stumbled onto the idea of forced hyper-efficiency and my dream schedule with a scheduling experiment I did for one month. **That one experiment changed my life** and opened my eyes to the power of experimenting.

In fact, **some of the best breakthroughs of my life have come from experiments.** For this reason, I've made experimenting a way of life, and always have at least one business or personal experiment I'm running.

I call this **"experiment your way to exceptional,"** where you keep optimizing various parts of your life so they keep getting better and better. I encourage you to do the same.

Here are some of the experiments that I've run in the past, just to give you some ideas:

- No social media for thirty days
- No technology past 6:00 p.m. for thirty days
- Eating only fruits, nuts, and vegetables for thirty days
- Only checking email three days per week for thirty days
- Deleting all apps from my phone except for the few essential apps like phone, text, and photos for thirty days. Then, carefully adding back only the bare essential ones.
- Meditating for at least ten minutes per day for thirty days.

I ran many of these experiments because I was starting to feel addicted to those technologies. Any time I notice a pattern that feels addicting, I like to set boundaries around it that are healthier. A great way to do this is with a 30-day experiment, because it somehow feels easier to commit to just thirty days versus making a permanent change.

So, after I completed the social media experiment, I only added back the Facebook app, and I moved the app icon on my phone so it's hard to find. I wanted to make sure I consciously decide that it's important for me to open the app in that particular moment. I found that I had become addicted to using it and felt that wasn't good for me.

As another example, I do the 30-day vegetarian cleanse once per year to help me lose weight, but also to help me ensure that I don't have a sugar or other food addiction (which I have struggled with in the past).

I also run experiments out of curiosity, like if I read something that says a certain activity will be beneficial. This is how I formed the habit of daily meditation. I initially started meditating as an experiment and then loved the results, so I made it a habit.

In fact, it was the meditation retreat that I shared with you in previous chapters that initially led me to doing the time experiment. So that first experiment (trying meditation) led me to another experiment (the time experiment), and here I am many years later a totally changed person as a result.

experiment your way to exceptional.

Take a moment right now and **write down some ideas for the types of experiments you might want to try.** Just brainstorm whatever comes to mind.

If you need help coming up with some ideas, I recommend you write down some of the principles that I've covered in this book to try as an experiment (which hopefully you plan to do anyway).

You can also refer to your Epic Life Plan that you created earlier and see what types of experiments might be interesting to try in each of the 8 categories of happiness.

I sometimes refer to my experiments as **"hacking the hack" where I try to uplevel my previous "best."** Feel free to ask me about my current experiment if you ever talk to me in person. Experimenting has become an obsession of mine.

I truly hope that you **adopt an experimenter's attitude for life** too and always have an experiment that you are running. When you do this, your life continues to get better and better. I promise!

Well, can you believe it? We're almost to the end of the book.

All that's left now is to recap everything you've learned and reflect on how far you've come on this journey with me.

Oh, yeah. And I'll finally tell you the most bizarre part of my house fire story that you'll simply never believe happened, and where to access some additional training if you like what I've covered here.

CONCLUSION
AND NEXT STEPS

You *can* have it all—business, growth, *and* plenty of free time. In fact, I believe it is your birthright. **You just have to decide to have freedom. Right here. Right now.**

I've given you the tools you need to make it happen if you truly want to. The only thing standing in your way is you.

Let's recap everything we've discussed so far and then go over my recommended next steps.

In Chapter 1, you learned about where **the Vacation Effect name** comes from, and how it has a double meaning. The first meaning is that you can become hyper-efficient like you are when you are about to go on vacation. The second meaning is that your life should have so much joy built in each week that it feels like a perpetual vacation.

In Chapters 2–4, you mapped out where you are right now and what **your epic life** will look like. You also identified some of those **"Someday Maybes"** that you keep saying you'd like to do someday.

In Chapter 5, you learned about the **Life Purpose Framework** that helps you identify or refine your life purpose into something powerful and tangible. You also discovered your **Power Word,** which summarizes your life purpose in a single word. Your Power Word can help you evaluate opportunities in the future and help you measure your progress.

In Chapters 6–9, you discovered **how to grow by subtraction** by removing stuff from your to-do list, not adding to it. You learned how to conduct your own 30-day experiment so you can find your own hyper-efficient sweet spot. You were armed with **9 growth and happiness multipliers** that you can use regularly to make growth by subtraction an automatic and permanent part of your life. You also learned how to implement a proper **Business Navigation System** to create explosive growth and make sure your business is on the right track.

Then in Chapter 10, you learned about what it means to **live the Vacation Effect Lifestyle** and the importance of combining everything you've learned in Chapters 2–9 to experience the compound effect of their overlapping synergies.

In Chapter 11, we covered how to **course correct when things go wrong,** because they will.

Then, in Chapter 12, you learned how to **adopt an experimenter's attitude** so that life continues to get better and better all the time.

As a reminder, I've also included a summary of the key concepts from the book, which I call a **Rocket Summary.** Please use the Rocket Summary any time you want a quick summary of these principles without having to dig for them.

So, **we sure have covered a lot of ground,** haven't we?

The techniques in Chapters 1–12 are the ones that I've personally used to transform my own life, and I'm so pleased to be here sharing them with you too.

In fact, I plan to use these techniques to have fun experimenting my way to exceptional for the rest of my life. For example, I plan to travel to all seven continents by the time I reach the age of fifty, and to spend plenty of Freedom Days doing the things I truly *love*, including exploring, hiking, and photography.

As a reminder, **when I mention Freedom Days, I'm talking about** *business days* (not weekends). I take Freedom Days off in addition to the weekends. I want to be able to look back on my life and say, *"Wow, I pretty much did it all."*

What about you?

When you look back on your life, what do you want to make sure you have accomplished?

You may recall that I had you go through this exercise back in Chapter 2. But now that you've finished the whole book, I wanted to revisit this since it is so important.

Please look back at what you wrote down before.

Did you write down that it was important for you to spend a lot of time working? Or did you write down that it was important that you spend a lot of time with the people and causes you really care about?

Be honest with yourself and really answer those questions if you didn't before.

And speaking of being honest...

I'm about to drop a real truth bomb on you here.

Are you ready?

Remember I told you at the beginning of the book how there was a crazy part of my house fire story that you'll probably never believe?

Well, here is the rest of that story. I know it will sound crazy, because I still can't believe it myself. But it really happened.

Let's roll back the clock to the year 2011. I had been following a nightly routine for six months where I would say my normal prayers, and then visualize a $3 million check payable to me that was dated June 20, 2011.

As part of my routine, while visualizing the check, I would also say a mantra (or prayer) in my head that was something like: *On June 20, 2011, at 8:00 a.m., I generate 3 million dollars.*

I kept repeating that mantra over and over again until I fell asleep, as I kept the image of the check in my mind.

June 20 at 8:00 a.m. was part of my visualization routine because I had a launch starting at that exact time for a new information product I was releasing. A lot of my clients who were scheduled to send out their promotions for my launch had generated $3 million from their own launches, so that was a goal I had made for myself too.

Well, instead of a three-million-dollar product launch, at exactly 8:00 a.m. on June 20, 2011—literally down to the exact second—**guess what happened instead?**

My house was struck by a bolt of lightning and caught fire. Instead of having a successful launch, I was literally putting out fires at that time.

But **here's the crazy part.** I'll bet you can guess what the insurance checks totaled up to be.

Yes, pretty much exactly what I had been visualizing.

But do you see the real problem here? **There was an error in my visualization logic.**

With a product launch, you don't normally get a seven-figure check. There are normally various transactions coming through that amount to $200 or $2,000 (or whatever your products cost). Those transactions can add up to seven figures in your bank account over one or multiple days as the sales are collected.

But **God responded to exactly what I had been asking for** over that six-month period very passionately with one of the only ways that would satisfy my request for a literal check like that.

So, **he sent me a lightning bolt.**

At the *exact* second I had asked for it to happen.

Is that crazy or what?

Yes, that really happened to me.

I still can't believe it myself every time I think about it.

Now my husband jokes with me from time to time and says, *"Denise, what are you visualizing as part of your nightly routine? Is it anything I need to be worried about?"*

All kidding aside, **this just demonstrates how powerful our intentions and prayers can be** and how important it is that we be careful about the details of our specific requests.

I'm certainly not perfect and have my own ups and downs, which I've told you about before.

But I've learned to use my intentions and the techniques in this book to **create an epic life for myself.**

And I've learned to get myself back on track whenever I deviate, and to always keep experimenting my way to a better version.

I truly hope these techniques help you create your own epic life. I'm including some recommendations below to help you accomplish that.

WHAT I RECOMMEND YOU DO NEXT

1. LEAVE A REVIEW ON AMAZON

If you found this book helpful, I'd be incredibly grateful if you would leave a five-star rating and/or a review on Amazon to let others know that you enjoyed it. I'm on a mission to transform the lives of over 10,000 business owners around the world, and when you take just a couple of minutes to leave a rating and review on Amazon, it lets other business owners know that this book is worth checking out.

2. WATCH MY PRIVATE BEHIND-THE-SCENES TRAINING THAT COVERS MY METHODOLOGY IN MORE DETAIL

If you're reading this book, it's because you're interested in growing your business and having more free time. I put together a free private training that goes into even more detail on how you can implement my methodologies on your own, and how you can work with me and my team if you would like our help doing so. You can sign up for it here: *DeniseGosnell. com/free-training-vip.*

3. APPLY TO JOIN THE VACATION EFFECT COACHING PROGRAM AND BECOME PART OF MY INNER CIRCLE

If you're serious about implementing the principles that I covered in this book within your business and life, and want me to provide you all the tools, worksheets, and guidance in making that happen, please join me in my coaching program. I have group coaching and one-on-one coaching programs available and even offer a results-based guarantee to help ensure that you succeed. You can apply at *DeniseGosnell.com/free-training-vip* and get all of the program details (including the free training mentioned above).

I also offer a digital course for those who don't want the coaching and accountability but still want the advanced training and templates. Once you apply, you can get more details about all the program levels.

4. WORK WITH ME DIRECTLY

If you'd like to hire me for private consulting, one-on-one coaching, or to have me speak at one of your events, you can learn more about how to work with me here: *DeniseGosnell.com/work-with-me*.

5. BUY MY OTHER BOOKS

I also have two additional books being published as part of the Vacation Effect series. They are called *The Vacation Effect for Teams* and *The Vacation Effect for Everyday Living*.

In **The Vacation Effect for Teams,** you can learn how to build hyper-efficient teams and create a culture where your employees are some of your biggest fans.

In *The Vacation Effect for Everyday Living*, you can learn about some of the general principles that I have used to transform my life as a human being, and that apply to everyone, whether you are an entrepreneur or not.

More details about these books can be found on my website at *DeniseGosnell.com/books*.

6. CHECK OUT MY WEBSITE FOR LOTS OF FREE RESOURCES

On my website at *DeniseGosnell.com*, you can find various articles, news that I've been featured in, and podcasts I've appeared in, sign up for my free training, join my mailing list, learn about my programs, and more.

7. FOLLOW ME ON SOCIAL MEDIA

If you'd like to stay connected on social media, you can do so here:

- Facebook: *Facebook.com/DeniseGosnellPage*
- LinkedIn: *LinkedIn.com/in/DeniseGosnell*

8. REACH OUT TO ME

Please reach out to me any time if I can help you, or to tell me which of these principles resonated with you the most.

You can connect with me at *dgosnell@denisegosnell.com* or through my website at *DeniseGosnell.com/contact*.

Helping busy entrepreneurs grow their business *and* have plenty of free time without having to choose one over the other is **what I do.**

Showing busy entrepreneurs how to create more freedom than they ever dreamed possible for what really matters in life is **who I am.**

That's why nothing would make me happier than knowing the principles in this book changed your life.

Freedom is a Mindset, Not a Destination™
You decide to have freedom.

ROCKET SUMMARY®

CHAPTER 1: INTRODUCING THE VACATION EFFECT

For six years after my house fire, **I tried about everything you can think of to figure out how to have growth in my business** *and* **plenty of free time.**

I attended a meditation retreat in 2017, where I received a message from the divine. *"All you have to do is decide and make today the way you want tomorrow to be."*

At that moment, **I decided to create the three-day work schedule I had always wanted as a 30-day experiment.** I blocked off Tuesdays and Thursdays as free days for the next month to do whatever I wanted that would make me happy.

During my little time experiment, **I learned that you can actually grow by subtraction by removing things from your to-do list.** Not by adding to it.

Have you ever noticed that when you get ready to go on vacation, you get as much done in the two days right before you leave as you normally do in like a month? Why is that? It's because you know that you won't be available due to the vacation, so **you force yourself to focus on what matters most.** This is what I refer to as "**forced hyper-efficiency.**"

With my little experiment, I was forcing myself to be hyper-efficient by only allowing myself to work in my businesses on Monday, Wednesday, and Friday.

It turns out that there was a **double benefit to this approach:** I became great at prioritizing and finishing the critical few projects that really mattered, while ignoring or delegating everything else.

Because of the Tuesday and Thursday free time I was giving myself, each week started to include so much joy, that **life felt like a perpetual vacation.**

Those two principles are what led me to the name: "**the Vacation Effect.**"

I also learned that **Freedom is a mindset, not a destination.** Freedom isn't a destination that you get to someday, when you reach a certain goal.

Freedom is a decision you make. You choose to have freedom.

After having the best year of my life in terms of revenue and happiness up until that point, others started asking me what I did. **So, I reverse engineered exactly what I did that worked,** and those principles are covered in the later chapters.

CHAPTER 2: THE HAPPINESS SCORECARD

You were asked to take a moment and **really think about your answers to these questions:**

- Am I truly happy with my life?
- If I died right now, would I be satisfied with how I've lived my life, or would I have a lot of regrets?

You were then asked to **rate your level of happiness in each of these 8 categories of happiness** on a scale of 1–12, with 1 being the lowest and 12 being the highest.

- Life Purpose
- Business and Career
- Time
- Money
- Relationships
- Wellness
- Home Environment
- Adventure

8 Categories of Happiness

When you achieve your best in a given category, I believe it is the greatest feeling of freedom you can have.

You were then given instructions on calculating and evaluating your Net Happiness Score, which is the total of your scores in each of the 8 categories.

You were also asked to **evaluate how well you are living in alignment with your true priorities.**

CHAPTER 3: QUIT LYING TO YOURSELF— IT'S TIME TO FACE YOUR SOMEDAY MAYBES

To me, **Someday Maybes are future joy that you're depriving yourself of** now for no good reason.

That's where you say to yourself: *"Someday, when I have more [time, money], I'll do [the thing I want to do]."*

Here are some examples:

- Someday, when I have more money, I'll travel to more places.
- Someday, when I have more time, I'll spend it with friends, family, and on causes I care about.

If you don't get around to doing those things that would bring you joy now, **when will you ever truly do them?**

Probably *never*, unless something drastic changes.

You were guided through some exercises to help you

If not now, then when?

bring your Someday Maybes into the now or give yourself permission to let them go.

CHAPTER 4: CREATING YOUR EPIC LIFE PLAN

You learned the importance of creating an overall plan for your "life," like you often do for your business.

You then mapped out **what you want your Epic Life to look like** in each of the 8 categories of happiness:

- Life Purpose
- Business and Career
- Time
- Money

- Relationships
- Wellness
- Home Environment
- Adventure

You were asked to answer the following questions about each of these eight areas:

- How did you rate yourself on the Happiness Scorecard for this category? Why did you assign that score?
- What do you really want (to be, do, feel, or have) in this category?
- What is the biggest obstacle standing in the way of where you are right now and where you would like to be in that category? What are some ways you can overcome that obstacle?

- What are the best actions you can take in the next month or quarter to move closer to that goal?

Your Epic Life Plan will become the roadmap for what to change in your business and what to do with all the free time you're about to create.

CHAPTER 5: IDENTIFYING YOUR LIFE PURPOSE AND POWER WORD

I believe the **life purpose** that God intended for each of us to experience is that we simply live in joy.

I also believe that the best way to live in joy is to **identify your unique talents that you love using and share them with the world.** The act of doing what you love and sharing it with others creates the joy.

I created the Life Purpose Framework to make this concept more tangible. There are three parts to the framework:

1. Identify your top three unique and joyful talents.
2. Find a Power Word (a single word) that summarizes your three main talents.
3. Create your Life Purpose Statement.

Here is the **formula for crafting your own Life Purpose Statement:**

I am a [Power Word]. I am at my best when I'm:

- [Unique Talent #1]
- [Unique Talent #2]
- [Unique Talent #3]

You can use your Power Word and Life Purpose Statement in your everyday life in a variety of ways, such as to help you pick hobbies, to evaluate whether to take on a new client or project, etc.

CHAPTER 6: HOW TO GROW BY SUBTRACTION

We covered how to **grow your business by doing less**, by removing from, not adding to your to-do list. This is what I refer to as **Grow by Subtraction**. It's about focusing on the critical few efforts that will produce the greatest results.

We learned about the **Pareto Principle**, and how 80 percent of your efforts generally only produce 20 percent of the results. The reverse is also said to be true, where 20 percent of your efforts are what generally produce 80 percent of the results.

One reason we don't operate this way all the time is because of the business culture that focuses on the grind, grind, grind mentality.

Sometimes the better answer is to stop doing something and take a different approach instead, or to simply do nothing at all.

There is also the problem of Parkinson's Law, where the time it takes to complete a project expands to the amount of time you have given yourself to complete it. The result is that practically everything takes longer than it should.

And then there's the guilt you feel—like you're somehow lazy—if you're not working all...the...time...

So how do we solve this problem of working harder, instead of smarter, when the odds are so deeply against us?

Here's how:

GROW BY SUBTRACTION AUTOMATICALLY AND PERMANENTLY

You **grow by subtraction** by focusing on just the 20 percent of projects that will produce 80 percent of the results.

You **make it automatic** by limiting the amount of time you are willing to spend on the projects, through what I called forced hyper-efficiency. This automatically forces you to focus on results versus time spent.

BY SUBTRACTION
automatically and permanently

You then **make this workflow permanent** by replacing your newfound free time with more joyful activities, so you never want to give them up.

CHAPTER 7: THE 30-DAY HYPER-EFFICIENCY EXPERIMENT

After receiving a crystal-clear message during a meditation retreat about the importance of making today what I want tomorrow to be, I did a scheduling experiment that would forever change my life.

I recommended that you do the same type of experiment for yourself where you take eight business days as Freedom Days for one month.

A **Freedom Day** is defined as a business day (not a weekend day) where you do things that bring you joy but are not *in* the trenches of your business. You can use this for personal time, creativity to work *on* the business, start a new business, or whatever makes you happy. Ideally, you will have nothing scheduled that day, so you can wake up and say, "What do I want to do today that will bring me the most joy?"

The purpose of this "30-Day Hyper-Efficiency Experiment" is twofold:

1. To help you identify some inefficiencies that will rise to the top when you force hyper-efficiency into your schedule (again, this is just temporary for the experiment). You can then optimize those inefficiencies one by one using the strategies we covered in Chapter 8.

2. To help you have more free time for those Someday Maybes and other things that will bring you joy, so you can experience what true freedom is like. In other words, it's also designed to help you work less and play more.

I then walked you through the process of designing your own experiment and overcoming the most common objections that come up.

If you see this experiment through, there is a beautiful land waiting on the other side with more joy, richness, and freedom than you have probably ever experienced in your life.

CHAPTER 8: MULTIPLIERS TO HELP YOU GROW BY SUBTRACTION AUTOMATICALLY

We covered nine strategies that you can combine to make growth by subtraction happen automatically and permanently. I call these strategies **The 9 Growth and Happiness Multipliers:**

- Multiplier #1: Forced Hyper-Efficiency
- Multiplier #2: Freedom Days and Happiness Stacking
- Multiplier #3: Goal Setting and Freedom Planning
- Multiplier #4: Time Hacking
- Multiplier #5: Success Rituals
- Multiplier #6: Effective Delegation and Outsourcing
- Multiplier #7: Standard Operating Procedures
- Multiplier #8: Advanced Systems and Automation
- Multiplier #9: Revenue and Expense Optimization

MULTIPLIER #1: FORCED HYPER-EFFICIENCY

Growth + Happiness Multipliers

With forced hyper-efficiency, you basically **limit the amount of time you're willing to work** in any given week. This forces you to focus on getting *results* with the time you spend, and to eliminate the stuff that doesn't matter.

MULTIPLIER #2: FREEDOM DAYS AND HAPPINESS STACKING

This is where you combine your Freedom Days with happiness stacking, where you do multiple things together that would make you happy.

MULTIPLIER #3: GOAL SETTING AND FREEDOM PLANNING

We covered four key goal-setting and planning strategies that are essential to continued growth:

- **Planning Strategy #1:** A system for making consistent progress on your Epic Life Plan
- **Planning Strategy #2:** A system for making consistent progress on implementing these nine multipliers
- **Planning Strategy #3:** An effective method for planning bigger goals and breaking them down into the steps that will lead to real results

- **Planning Strategy #4:** An effective strategy for deciding how to spend your time each day on things that produce real results

MULTIPLIER #4: TIME HACKING

I then included a detailed list of some of **my favorite time hacks** and explained when you might use them, including my powerful process for identifying the biggest levers that you should work on first.

MULTIPLIER #5: SUCCESS RITUALS

A success ritual is an activity that you work into your daily routine **that will add up over time to a desired result.** I recommended that you tie your goals to success rituals whenever possible so you can succeed automatically, without needing a lot of willpower.

MULTIPLIER #6: EFFECTIVE DELEGATION AND OUTSOURCING

I explained the importance of delegation and shared a **delegation process** that I follow when I task things to my team:

- The project description
- What does success look like?
- The priority/deadline
- Level of creative leeway
- Level of authority

- Is there an existing policy or procedure they should follow?

I **also covered three outsourcing hacks** that I often use and recommend that you use as well.

MULTIPLIER #7: STANDARD OPERATING PROCEDURES (SOPS)

A great way to give yourself incredible freedom is to clone yourself and what you know so others can carry that out even when you aren't working. You should also capture the knowledge of other key roles in your company.

The best way to capture this knowledge is **through standard operating procedures,** such as for the following areas:

- Marketing/Client Attraction
- Sales/Client Enrollment
- Delivery of Client Work
- Team
- Office Environment
- Money/Business Metrics

MULTIPLIER #8: ADVANCED SYSTEMS AND AUTOMATION

You learned about **four different types of automation:** people automation, template automation, software automation, and hardware automation. You learned several examples of how to use each one of these to make your business more streamlined.

MULTIPLIER #9: REVENUE AND EXPENSE OPTIMIZATION

We covered several ways you can **increase your revenue and cut your expenses**. This is an important strategy for you to revisit periodically so you can really optimize the profitability and growth of your business over the long term.

CHAPTER 9: IMPLEMENTING A PROPER BUSINESS NAVIGATION SYSTEM

You learned about the importance of having a Business Navigation System that allows you to **track the progress and health of your overall business** and make sure the right projects get done in the right order.

Your Business Navigation System should include these key features, plus any others that make sense for your business:

- An organized way to track your goals, projects, and tasks
- A process for keeping everyone accountable and focused on the "right" projects
- Tracking of your key performance indicators

CHAPTER 10: LIVING THE VACATION EFFECT LIFESTYLE

You learned what it means to live "the Vacation Effect Lifestyle." There is a compound effect that happens when you combine the principles in this book.

Less Work + Forced Hyper-Efficiency + More Joy = Faster Business Growth

When you live the Vacation Effect Lifestyle, life has so much joy built in that **each week feels like a vacation.** When you do this correctly you get faster business growth.

This is what I referred to in earlier chapters as **grow by subtraction automatically and permanently.**

CHAPTER 11: COURSE CORRECTING WHEN THINGS GO WRONG

The Vacation Effect Lifestyle is certainly great, **but that doesn't mean life will always be perfect.** There will always be a few curve balls headed your way.

You learned about The Freedom Day Protector to help you evaluate whether or not to throw more of your personal time and/or resources at a project.

The Freedom Day Protector includes the following:

- **Part 1. Evaluating who should handle the crisis:**
  You determine whether or not this is something you personally need to handle. If yes, you go to Part 2, and if not, you skip to Part 3.

- **Part 2. It needs to be handled by me personally:** Here, you evaluate whether throwing more of your own time and resources will truly solve the program, and whether giving up your Freedom Days would really solve it.
- **Part 3. It needs to be handled by a team member:**
  If you aren't the best person to handle the issue, you then identify what person on your team should be, and whether or not they have the resources they need to handle it.

I highly recommend that you **use the Freedom Day Protector to help guard your Freedom Days** as much as possible. When it is truly necessary to deviate and work extra to handle a crisis that demands your personal attention, just do so. And don't feel guilty about it. Then get back to taking those days off again as soon as you can.

CHAPTER 12: EXPERIMENT YOUR WAY TO EXCEPTIONAL

I shared several examples of how **some of the best breakthroughs of my life have come from experiments.** For this reason, I've made experimenting a way of life, and always have at least one business or personal experiment I'm running.

LIFE IS A SERIES OF WONDERFUL EXPERIMENTS

experiment your way to exceptional.

I call this **"experiment your way to exceptional,"** where you keep optimizing various parts of your life, so they keep getting better and better. I encourage you to do the same.

CONCLUSION AND NEXT STEPS

I've personally used the techniques covered in Chapters 1–12 to transform my own life, and I'm so pleased to have shared them with you too.

I want to be able to look back on my life and say, *"Wow, I pretty much did it all."* Don't you?

I then shared the craziest part of my house fire story and how I created the exact result that I had been visualizing for the six months before it happened, even though it didn't come in the way I expected.

I learned the importance of being crystal clear in what

you are asking for, so you don't get such an unexpected result like I did.

I've also learned to use my intentions and the techniques in this book to create an epic life for myself. And, to get myself back on track whenever I deviate. I always keep experimenting my way to a better version. I truly hope these techniques help you create your own epic life.

I then shared my recommended next steps to help you on your journey.

RECOMMENDED NEXT STEPS

1. LEAVE A REVIEW ON AMAZON

If you found this book helpful, I'd be incredibly grateful if you would leave a five-star rating and/or a review on Amazon to let others know that you enjoyed it.

2. WATCH MY PRIVATE BEHIND-THE-SCENES TRAINING THAT COVERS MY METHODOLOGY IN MORE DETAIL

You can apply for access to my private training with details on how to implement my methodologies yourself or hire me and my team to help you. You can sign up for it here: *DeniseGosnell. com/free-training-vip.*

3. APPLY TO JOIN THE VACATION EFFECT COACHING PROGRAM AND BECOME PART OF MY INNER CIRCLE

If you'd like to work with me in one of my coaching programs or learn about my digital course, you can apply at *DeniseGosnell.*

com/free-training-vip and get all of the program details (including the free training mentioned above).

4. WORK WITH ME DIRECTLY

At *DeniseGosnell.com/work-with-me*, you can learn more about how to hire me for private consulting, one-on-one coaching, or have me speak at one of your events.

5. BUY MY OTHER BOOKS

I also have two additional books being published as part of the Vacation Effect series. They are called *The Vacation Effect for Teams* and *The Vacation Effect for Everyday Living*.

More details about these books can be found on my website at *DeniseGosnell.com/books*.

6. CHECK OUT MY WEBSITE FOR LOTS OF FREE RESOURCES

Check out *DeniseGosnell.com* for various articles, news, and other free resources.

7. FOLLOW ME ON SOCIAL MEDIA

Connect with me on social media here:

- Facebook: *Facebook.com/DeniseGosnellPage*
- LinkedIn: *LinkedIn.com/in/DeniseGosnell*

8. REACH OUT TO ME

You can connect with me at *dgosnell@denisegosnell.com* or through my website at *DeniseGosnell.com/contact*.

Helping busy entrepreneurs grow their business *and* have plenty of free time without having to choose one over the other is **what I do.**

Showing busy entrepreneurs how to create more freedom than they ever dreamed possible for what really matters in life is **who I am.**

Freedom is a Mindset, Not a Destination™
You decide to have freedom.

THE VACATION EFFECT® COACHING PROGRAM

BUILD A STREAMLINED BUSINESS AND LIVE THE VACATION EFFECT LIFESTYLE!

 Imagine having Denise Gosnell's personal guidance and accountability on creating a streamlined business with tons more free time. Denise is a trusted advisor to several of today's world-renowned thought leaders and business owners, and now you can get access to her incredible wisdom too.

This program includes all the coaching, accountability, tools, templates, and shortcuts for transforming your business into one that runs without your daily presence, while allowing you to live the Vacation Effect Lifestyle.

- Finally create a freedom lifestyle without sacrificing your business growth.
- Streamline your business into a well-oiled machine that runs without your daily involvement.
- Receive guidance and accountability from Denise and her team to accelerate your success.
- Denise is so confident in these powerful methods that she offers a results-based guarantee to ensure your success.

LIMITED SPOTS ARE AVAILABLE. APPLY TODAY!

DeniseGosnell.com/free-training-vip

HAVE DENISE SPEAK AT YOUR NEXT EVENT

Denise has spoken on stages in eight countries around the world over the past twenty-five-plus years on various topics ranging from business strategy and freedom lifestyle design to legal, technology, real estate, and more.

- Stop waiting for "someday" to create the life you've been dreaming of.
- Carve out a ton more freedom to spend on the things that really matter to you.
- Optimize your business so it runs like a well-oiled machine, and gets you better positioned to sell it in the future if you want to.

Denise will motivate and captivate your audience to create greater wealth, abundance, and freedom in their lives.

BOOK DENISE TODAY FOR YOUR NEXT EVENT.
DeniseGosnell.com/speaking

THE VACATION EFFECT® MASTERCLASS

LEARN THESE ADVANCED STRATEGIES IN JUST ONE HOUR!

Join Denise in a free behind-the-scenes training that covers the following:

- Denise's three-part framework for creating a streamlined business and taking a lot more time off.
- The pitfalls to look out for if you try to implement the three-part framework on your own.
- How to create the life you want today, not someday when you have more time or more money.
- How to free up one to two days per week (if you want) within ninety days and still grow your business by 10–30 percent or more each year.
- How to build a company that runs without your constant presence (so you can take more time off or sell it one day).
- The four types of business owners, and what to do depending on which category you fall into.
- Details on how you can work with Denise and her team if you want help implementing these principles in your business and life.

Apply today at *DeniseGosnell.com/free-training-vip.*